Objectivity: A Very Short Introduction

VERY SHORT INTRODUCTIONS are for anyone wanting a stimulating
and accessible way into a new subject. They are written by experts, and
have been translated into more than 45 different languages.

The series began in 1995, and now covers a wide variety of topics in
every discipline. The VSI library now contains over 500 volumes—a Very
Short Introduction to everything from Psychology and Philosophy of
Science to American History and Relativity—and continues to grow in every
subject area.

Titles in the series include the following:

Stephen Gaukroger

OBJECTIVITY

A Very Short Introduction

OXFORD
UNIVERSITY PRESS

OXFORD
UNIVERSITY PRESS

Great Clarendon Street, Oxford ox2 6DP

Oxford University Press is a department of the University of Oxford.
It furthers the University's objective of excellence in research, scholarship,
and education by publishing worldwide in

Oxford New York

Auckland Cape Town Dar es Salaam Hong Kong Karachi
Kuala Lumpur Madrid Melbourne Mexico City Nairobi
New Delhi Shanghai Taipei Toronto

With offices in

Argentina Austria Brazil Chile Czech Republic France Greece
Guatemala Hungary Italy Japan Poland Portugal Singapore
South Korea Switzerland Thailand Turkey Ukraine Vietnam

Oxford is a registered trade mark of Oxford University Press
in the UK and in certain other countries

Published in the United States
by Oxford University Press Inc., New York

British Library Cataloguing in Publication Data

Data available

Library of Congress Cataloging in Publication Data

Data available

Typeset by SPI Publisher Services, Pondicherry, India
Printed and bound by
CPI Group (UK) Ltd, Croydon, CR0 4YY

ISBN 978-0-19-960669-6

Contents

Chapter 1
Introduction: the varieties of objectivity

Objectivity is a distinctively human trait, as only human beings have the capacity for objectivity. Over the centuries, in debates about what it is that marks out humans from animals, consideration has been given to rationality, consciousness, self-consciousness, free will, and morality. All have been challenged. Indeed, recent studies of non-human primates suggest that such qualities are not exclusive to humans. But objectivity involves the ability to shift perspective, and no one has ever attributed this to animals. Objectivity requires us to stand back from our perceptions, our beliefs and opinions, to reflect on them, and subject them to a particular kind of scrutiny and judgement. Above all, it requires a degree of indifference in judging that may conflict with our needs and desires. Yet objectivity has assumed an unassailable status. Values that have come to be associated with objectivity, such as impartiality and freedom from prejudice, now not only guide scientific enquiry, but have also been imported into the moral and political realms. They are now regarded as underpinning notions of fairness and equality. In other words, objectivity is not only distinctive of human reasoning and behaviour, it has been built into distinctively human goals and aspirations. In the modern era, it has become sought for its own sake, a value in its own right: something regularly contrasted with religious beliefs, for example.

This development dates from no earlier than the start of the 19th century, when the West's conception of its superiority shifted from its religion – Christianity – to its science. At issue here was not so much technological achievements, since the bulk of these were still to come, but an emerging package of values placing special emphasis on such ideals as meritocracy and freedom from prejudice. Objectivity lay at the core of this package, and science was seen to embody objectivity in its purest form. The historical context is important here. It is not difficult to see how objectivity is a matter of concern for those working in disciplines such as history and law, where something is needed to guide our interpretations of texts or events, or science, where we might need something to guide our experiments and our interpretation of results. But how can objectivity have become a matter of general concern, and above all, how could it be relevant to everyday moral, aesthetic, religious, or political decisions? What has happened is that something that was distinctive only of certain technical forms of enquiry has been transformed into a general constraint on all deliberations. The values that have come to be associated with objectivity, such as impartiality and lack of bias, have not only been seen as guiding scientific enquiry, but have been extrapolated into the social and political realms, underpinning notions of fairness and equality.

Here we face a important problem in our own culture's aspirations to objectivity. Its pre-eminence as a goal has resulted in other values masquerading as it, despite their having no relation to it and, in fact, serving to usurp genuinely objective judgements. What is often referred to as 'number-crunching' – the reduction of decision-making to quantification and measurement, and the exclusion of anything that cannot be treated in these terms – is a prime culprit here. Appeals to objectivity have been used to vindicate a culture of management in which targets are set so that standardized results can be generated, statistically analysed, and compared. Such practices are not necessarily subjected either to reasoned judgement or to the empirical evaluation of particular cases, but typically bypass any form of independent or objective reasoning at all. The idea that decision-making can be mechanized trades on a fundamental misunderstanding of objectivity, namely that it consists in removing, as far as possible, all elements of judgement from the interpretation of data. This supposedly eliminates individual prejudices and biases from interpretation and decision-making, offering something untouched by human brains, as it were. This is a widespread misunderstanding and a dangerous one. A recent example is the rejection, in government circles, of thinking about what universities should be teaching in favour of a model of consumer (student) choice. Competition theory suggests that consumer demand will produce judgement-free results, without reflection on the aims of pedagogy and education in our culture, and their role in fostering the values of our civilization. A methodology that bypasses the assumptions, values, and beliefs that inevitably accompany the exercise of judgement thereby makes claims to neutrality and objectivity. Standardized decision-making procedures stand in for reflection on the nature of the problem for which the decision is sought in the first place. Wholly misconstruing the nature of objectivity, they employ pseudo-scientific means of bypassing understanding and evaluation in favour of something that is deemed to transcend bias and prejudgement.

What is objectivity?

It seems natural that such a basic idea as objectivity would have a generally agreed meaning, so that our first step should be to set out a clear, core definition of objectivity, using it to identify misunderstandings. If only things were so simple! Objectivity, alas, is not a straightforward concept. Many difficulties are generated in the search for a definition, because 'objectivity' can be understood in different ways. Different expectations arise as a result – some are reasonable, some not. These difficulties are compounded by the fact that the different understandings of the term, and the different expectations they generate, are not wholly independent of one another.

Our first task is, then, to identify some of the more significant understandings of objectivity, indicate how they differ, and to try to capture what motivates them. These understandings will not necessarily be incompatible with one another, and they will usually be open to stronger or weaker formulations, but our primary purpose here is to get a sense of what is at stake: fine-tuning can wait until later.

The first understanding of objectivity is perhaps the most common one. It is that an objective judgement is a judgement that is free of prejudice and bias. One might put this by saying that it is a judgement to which any fair-minded person could agree, no matter what views they held. 'Fair-minded' and 'objective' are interdefinable here to some extent – to be objective is to be fair-minded, and to be fair-minded is to be objective – and this is enlightening. It locates objectivity in a social realm of everyday life, by contrast with that of science, for example. The idea of science, with its rigorous empirical testing, as embodying standards of objectivity is not a core notion in this idea of objectivity. We don't think of scientists as instituting standards of 'fairness', and the struggle for objectivity in science is hardly a matter of contemporary physicists and chemists freeing themselves from prejudice. There are accounts of science that take it as embodying universal canons of objectivity, which are then extrapolated to other realms of life – a 'scientific ethics' was popular in Britain in the 1920s and 1930s, for example. But if one thinks of objectivity as freedom from prejudice, then such an extrapolation, far from appearing natural, will be something whose appropriateness one will want to question. The idea of objectivity as freedom from prejudice and bias, while not irrelevant to science, seems somewhat marginal to its concerns as we now understand them. At the other end of spectrum, it provides some hope in applying standards of objectivity to ethical and aesthetic judgements, for example, and perhaps even to religion, although this is far more problematic. We shall return to these questions. For the moment, what I want to draw attention to is the fact that how we think of objectivity depends a great deal on where we locate its primary application. A notion devised to cover everyday life might have relevance problems when we come to consider science, and it might have application problems when we come to consider aesthetic judgements. Nevertheless, the idea of freedom from prejudice and bias may still be the most powerful general notion of objectivity that we have. I shall be arguing that this is in fact the case, and that it can be complemented by compatible but differently focused notions, especially when we turn to science, on the one hand, and ethics and aesthetics, on the other.

The second understanding is that an objective judgement is a judgement which is free of all assumptions and values. On the face of it, this looks like an extension of the idea of removing prejudices and bias. After all, one might argue, who is to say that the views we hold are prejudices and biases? Surely the sensible thing is to exclude all beliefs that we bring to a judgement, whether *we* consider them as prejudices or not. But the one is not merely an extension of the other, and there is a clear conceptual difference between them. The idea of prejudices and biases carries connotations of distortion, whereas that of assumptions and values need not. One way to think of the difference is that, in the first case, those things which one brings to a judgement that are not shared should be removed if the judgement is to be objective, whereas in the second case, the claim is that those things which one brings to a judgement, whether shared or not, should be removed if the judgement is to be objective. The difference is absolutely crucial because many sceptical and relativist arguments against the possibility of objectivity conflate the first and second understandings, so that the (achievable) task of removing all prejudices from arguments is treated as if it were the (unachievable) task of removing all assumptions.

The idea that we should aim to remove prejudices from our decisions might be difficult to realize in some cases (though not as difficult as it is sometimes made out), but the idea of a prejudice-free judgement makes perfectly good sense. By contrast, that we should aim to remove all prior beliefs is not merely impossible to realize, the idea does not stand up to scrutiny. This issue is the most important that we shall be dealing with, because it is the one with the gravest consequences.

The third notion of objectivity is focused directly on how we arrive at our views or theories. It is that an objective procedure is one that allows us to decide between conflicting views or theories. Whereas the first two notions set out to describe a particular state of mind – one free of prejudices or one free of any assumptions – to which we must aspire if we are to be objective, this notion does something different. It dictates that procedures of a particular kind must be in place and must be followed if we are to achieve objectivity, namely ones that enable us to decide between theories that conflict with one another. This is very much a notion that finds its home territory in science, and it was used, for example, by the philosopher Karl Popper, who effectively equated objectivity and science, to rule out history as an objective discipline. His argument was that in science our hypotheses have empirically different consequences, so we can check these against what actually happens. In history, by contrast, the relevant facts are always before us when we construct our hypotheses, so we cannot test them against the facts. What is the general principle at stake here? It is that objectivity requires us to devise procedures to decide between competing judgements in order to discover which makes factually correct predictions, and that we must prefer that which makes factually correct predictions. This cannot be all there is to objectivity, however. How the predictions are made and tested surely also raise questions of objectivity. There are in fact a range of other questions about interpretation of results, and of the content of the theories that are being compared, which, as we shall see, mean that comparing predictions turns out to be not at all straightforward, even in science. But here, what I want to draw attention to is the fact that in this case we have something more like a proposed necessary condition of objectivity, rather than a definition of objectivity *per se*. That is, this criterion does not tell us what objectivity is, as the first two understandings do, but rather proposes something we must do if we are to secure objectivity. But this does not make it an added extra. It is not something we must do if we are to secure objectivity *however understood*, because it imposes significant constrains on how one understands objectivity. For one thing, it is tied up with an understanding of objectivity which takes scientific objectivity as a general model, and this is a very substantive assumption. Second, this is reinforced by the fact that, if it is indeed a necessary condition for objectivity, then anything that lacks a means for deciding between views cannot be objective. In short, what we are looking at with this understanding of objectivity is a procedure that we must follow if we are to proceed in an objective fashion in science. It only becomes a general procedure if one thinks one can extrapolate from decision-making in science to decision-making generally. Popper thought one could, but the price paid is that nothing outside science comes out as objective: serious history and political propaganda come out as effectively equal, for example.

The 'decision' criterion aims to provide us with a procedure for deciding between competing hypotheses. It cannot establish that one of these is true, only which we should prefer relative to the evidence. Both hypotheses might turn out to be false: it is just that the evidence that would show them both to be false may not be revealed by this particular test. In fact, none of the understandings that we have examined up to now would enable us to establish the truth of a hypothesis. To see why, consider the standard definition of knowledge, due originally to Plato. This states that knowledge is justified true belief. Justified belief isn't enough for knowledge, on Plato's view, because justification is relative to the evidence. The history of science is littered with justified false theories: before the 16th century, the rotation of the Sun and the planets around the Earth had more justification – observational and theoretical – than the theory that the Sun was at the centre of our system. Similarly with true but unjustified theories: if I believe that the Earth is roughly spherical because it is the eyeball of a giant cosmic elephant, then I have a true belief, that the Earth is roughly spherical, but I cannot be said to know it, because my reasons for believing it are false. So, truth and justification are different things. On the views of objectivity that we have looked at up to now, the first (lack of prejudice) and the third (some procedure to decide between competing hypotheses) have taken objectivity to be a matter of justification, not truth. Objectivity is something that you must aspire to if you want your views to be justified. The second is a bit more ambiguous, since one direction that the 'no assumptions' argument might go in is to claim that, if we do away with all interpretations and assumptions, then we finally see things as they really are, independently of any subjective preconceptions we might bring to the judgement. That would connect truth and objectivity.

This has been generally recognized by philosophers as a problematic move and is not the route that has much traffic since the heyday of logical positivism. But philosophers have nevertheless been inclined to bring truth into the discussion of objectivity at a fundamental level, to tie truth and objectivity together. One could of course maintain that an approach is objective if it seeks the truth, where the aim might be described, as Aristotle put it, as 'saying of what is that it is, and of what is not that it is not', but this makes seeking the truth automatically a question of objectivity, which is implausible. There are any number of ways in which I might seek the truth, from reading tea-leaves to smashing particles into one another in an accelerator. They are hardly all objective. The connection has to be established in a different way, and we shall be focusing on the idea of 'accurate representation'.

This is the fourth understanding of objectivity, and in philosophical and scientific discussions from the 18th century onwards, we find a move away from a negative understanding of objectivity as freedom from prejudice or bias, towards the positive idea that objectivity consists in accurate representation. There are a number of fundamental differences between this conception and the lack of prejudice and lack of assumptions conceptions. The striking difference is that it offers what might be called a positive theory of objectivity. That is, it does not claim that we should remove something from our judgements if they are to aspire to objectivity, but rather that they need to be pointed in the right direction, so to speak. While the negative conceptions distance objectivity from truth, the positive one brings the two together in an apparent area of overlap, for accurate representation can be thought of both in terms of truth and in terms of objectivity.

The objectivity as accurate representation approach can be thought of as being motivated by two sets of considerations. The first is that we cannot make sense of objectivity without bringing in truth, because once we ask why we want to be objective in the first place, what role it serves, then the answer is that the whole point of objectivity is to reveal the truth. If objectivity and justification were not directed at truth, they wouldn't be objectivity and justification. The second is that, confining ourselves to objectivity in science, the role of objectivity in science is to enable it to provide an accurate representation of the world. I shall be arguing that both of these considerations are mistaken. As regards the first, truth in any substantive sense is just not the kind of thing that could guide scientific enquiry. On the second point, we shall be looking at practical issues in representation in science, and we shall see that 'accurate representation' raises questions of judgement not questions of truth. In short, I shall be arguing that objectivity plays an important role in scientific knowledge, for example, but this is because it strengthens and secures the justification requirement, not because it has anything to do with the truth requirement.

There is one final understanding of objectivity that needs to be considered briefly. This is the idea that something is objective if it leads to conclusions which are universally accepted. Part of the motivation for this idea is that when one considers results in the natural sciences, for example, there is a very significant level of agreement, a level of agreement that cuts across cultures, religions, and just about any other kind of cognitive endeavour. But this is at best a test of, or sign of, objectivity, not a definition of what objectivity is. Note, however, that it cannot be objected to this notion that there are periods in the history of science when there has been near universal agreement on a theory, such as geocentrism, which turned out to be wrong. This is irrelevant if objectivity is a matter of justification rather than truth. It would be a different matter if there were periods in which there had been universal agreement despite the evidence: then universal agreement would not be a sign of objectivity. One can make up stories where this would be the case, but I know of no such cases in reality where this can plausibly be maintained. The problem lies rather in 'universal' agreement, for there are always dissenting voices.

In sum, from among the conceptions I have outlined, we shall be examining three as contenders for general accounts of objectivity: that the judgement or theory should be prejudice-free, that it should be assumption-free, and that it should be an accurate representation. The claim that objective accounts should enable us to decide between alternatives can only be taken as a proposed necessary condition for objectivity, not an account of what objectivity is. Similarly, the 'universal consent' can only be taken as a proposed sign of objectivity, not an account of what objectivity is. Of the three general accounts, each can hold in both the everyday or the scientific cases, although the second and third are more closely modelled on the scientific case. Possibly as a result of this, the second and third are more problematic if we want to apply notions of objectivity in ethics and aesthetics, but these are particularly difficult cases anyway, as we shall see, and if objectivity as something assumption-free, or as accurate representation, turned out to be an inappropriate notion in the context of ethics or aesthetics, this wouldn't necessarily be a decisive factor.

It will be clear from what I have already said it would not be fruitful to propose a definition of objectivity, and then to test it against competing definitions. Different, sometimes incompatible, things are expected of objectivity, and, as I have indicated, seeking conceptions of objectivity that work primarily for science, for everyday concerns, and for social, moral and aesthetic questions may well lead us in different directions. What would be most useful would be a general conception of objectivity that was sensitive to the special demands of science on the one hand, and to those of the moral and aesthetic realms on the other. Supplementary considerations can then be introduced in these areas enabling us to show how and why the form that objectivity takes differs – in its specific goals, in how we recognize it, in what we require of it – while still leaving us with a sense that there is some core to the idea of objectivity, important if we are to understand why we value objectivity as a general desideratum.

This is an ideal, one which we are unlikely to satisfy in every respect. But the important thing is that we increase our understanding of the issues, even if we do not resolve all of them. We will learn that what scientists require of objectivity, in the context of representing the world, is something instrumental rather than something absolute: not that it meet demands of truth, but rather that it meet those of reliability. We will learn that what we require of objectivity in making everyday decisions has little to do with stripping our beliefs of judgements and interpretations so as to make them more factual, but with improving our judgements, which often means adding more interpretation, not less. In this way, as we shall see, science and everyday decisions are closer in what they require of objectivity than might initially be thought. Finally, as far as moral and aesthetic judgements are concerned, we shall see that rather different considerations hold, and to the extent to which objectivity can be secured in these cases, they cannot be assimilated.

In the chapters that follow, I have tried to identify a series of questions, questions that in some cases readers may already have asked themselves, which provide different problem contexts in which the issues can be explored in a specific way. I begin, in Chapter 2, by looking at the claim that a general feature of objectivity, one that establishes its standing as a central cultural value, is that it is a form of intellectual honesty. In Chapter 3, I examine developments in science sometimes thought to show that everything is relative to the observer, and hence that objectivity is impossible. Chapters 4 and 5 explore the connections between freedom from prejudice or bias, and the attempt to remove any assumptions from our reasoning. In Chapter 6, I focus on the question of how we are to understand scientific representations of the world. In Chapter 7, I look at the connection between objectivity and numerical presentation. Finally, in the last three chapters, I look at what objectivity might amount to in the human or social sciences, in ethics, and in aesthetics.

Chapter 2
Is objectivity a form of honesty?

In a recent interview, Larry Sanger, the co-founder of Wikipedia, describes the attitude of many of those working to build up Wikipedia in terms of a

> complete disregard for expert opinion among a group of amateurs working on a subject, and in particular...their tendency to openly express contempt for experts. There was this attitude that experts should be disqualified [from participating] by the very fact that they had published on the subject – that because they had published, they were therefore biased.

This is a surprising view: as if scientists, for example, were not qualified to write on science because the large amount of research they have published makes them biased. It is such an odd thing to believe, that one suspects that part of the problem is that something at least marginally more plausible has been formulated badly. It will help, if we are to uncover what might lie behind this view, if we can capture the motivation behind it.

The initiators of Wikipedia set out to provide a cumulative, open-source reference resource, quite different from the traditional reference volumes. Rather than attempting to offer definitive canonical statements by experts, it opened up its resources to anyone who cared to contribute (while indicating where the information offered needed to be backed up further). Because it was an open-access electronic resource, entries could be revised at any time by anybody, and it could draw on a vast number of informants who, in many cases, had extensive knowledge of an area, no matter how arcane, but would never have been involved in compiling more traditional reference works. We might think of such a project not as identifying 'experts' in advance, but rather opening up the resource and letting a process of accumulation and sifting occur. The final product comes from a process of self-correction, a process which, in the case of an electronic medium, is extremely rapid. The traditional procedure of putting out regular new print editions of reference works could not possibly have operated starting from scratch and proceeding via a process of accumulation and filtering. The internet opened up a new way of doing things and rapidly proved how effective such a procedure could be.

One thing at issue here is the question of authority. On the face of it, the contrast is between reference sources written by people identified as authorities, and those written simply by people who have an interest in the subject. But there is something misleading about this contrast. If the latter were what was at issue, then Wikipedia would simply be a series of blogs. For it to work as a reference source, we do not want to know what anybody at all thinks, but what someone who is well-informed about the subject matter thinks. And we want what that person writes to be balanced. Well-informed and balanced articles are what, in the main, we get in Wikipedia, and this is what helps make it the single most consulted reference source throughout the world.

The difference between a traditional reference work and Wikipedia is not, then, that one is biased and the other not. But nor is it that the traditional reference work argues from the authority of the author whereas, in Wikipedia, authority emerges from the product rather than from the standing of the person who wrote the entry. We expect objectivity of both, and the same kind of objectivity at that, and in neither case is it simply a question of authorial authority. Printed reference sources are assessed on much the same grounds as electronic ones: it is just that the time scale is very different. Huge numbers of books purporting to be authoritative have been published, but they have almost all become obsolete, those remaining having achieved authoritative status because they have withstood the test of time.

This does not mean that questions of authority are irrelevant to those of objectivity. In fact, modern notions of objectivity emerged very much in response to a crisis in conceptions of authority and reliability. Since these modern notions did not just redefine or clarify objectivity, but at the same time pushed it to the fore as a core value of modern culture, issues central to the modern understanding of objectivity are tied up in the conditions of its emergence.

Objectivity and intellectual morality

The promotion of objectivity to a quasi-moral value is driven largely by its identification with intellectual honesty. The idea of intellectual honesty has been critical in philosophy from Socrates and Plato onwards, and it received a new formulation in the 17th century, when it became associated with notions of freedom from bias, freedom from prejudice, and objectivity. Indeed, it became associated with these to such an extent that intellectual honesty and objectivity have become largely identified. Yet intellectual honesty carries quasi-moral overtones, whereas objectivity, in its own right, does not. The identification of the two transforms objectivity into something that goes beyond the specifics of its application in particular disciplines. It becomes a general cultural value.

The issue of intellectual honesty arises in the first discussion we have of what it is to be a philosopher, in Plato's early dialogues, where Socrates is the personification of the idea of philosopher. In the dialogues, Socrates encounters what might be described as amateur and professional debaters. The former are just his friends and acquaintances, whereas the latter come under the generic heading of 'sophists', and they are experts – usually paid – at arguing. They are a little like modern barristers, with a similar aim, to find the best arguments for a case, whether it be at court or in a political assembly. Moreover, they teach these skills for a fee. But they are not true philosophers. What marks them out from a true philosopher such as Socrates in Plato's dialogues is not Socrates' greater skill at arguing. Rather, it is what motivates the argument in the first place. Philosophy is about conviction by means of argument, but the example of the sophist is intended to show that there must be more to it than that. The sophist is characterized as someone who is concerned simply to win arguments, without regard to the truth or falsity of the conclusion, whereas the philosopher is someone who uses argument to discover the truth of things. This extra quality that the philosopher must have came to be termed 'intellectual honesty' by Aristotle, Plato's pupil. One respect in which sophists' arguments were especially objectionable to Plato was in the domain of morals. Plato's main aim was to instill virtue into rulers. Because sophists were not concerned to discover the truth, they treated morality as if it were at best merely conventional and at worst subjective. Here intellectual honesty directly serves moral aims. More generally the same considerations are relevant to any form of inquiry.

In the 16th and 17th centuries, it was 'scholastic' philosophers – clerics who taught philosophy in a highly regulated way in the universities – who were slotted into the role once filled by the sophists, and they were criticized for pursuing sterile argument for its own sake, without regard to any productive outcome, and specifically without regard to truth. The scholastic philosophers were followers of Aristotle, and they were particularly taken to task by advocates of the new sciences of the 17th century. The connection between intellectual honesty and objectivity begins to be established at this time. Galileo, for example, charged his opponents with having pre-conceived ideas, construed as a form of vested interests, and Aristotelians are presented as people with an axe to grind, unable to argue a case on its merits and so having to rely on a philosophical system, which is treated as a form of intellectual dishonesty and a lack of objectivity. Reflecting on such issues, Robert Hooke, the great English scientist from the late 17th century, talks of the ideal observer being 'in no ways prejudiced or byassed by Interest, affection, hatred, fear or hopes'. This echoes Montaigne's comment on ideal observers, a century earlier. 'The man I had,' he tells us, 'was a simple crude fellow – a character fit to bear true witness; for clever people observe more things and more curiously, but they interpret them; and to lend weight and conviction to their interpretation, they cannot help altering history a little…We need a man very honest, or so simple that he has not the stuff to build up false inventions and give them plausibility; and wedded to no theory. Such was my man.'

In the 18th century, the association of objectivity with intellectual honesty was firmly established, and was being used by French thinkers in the defence of science and the disparagement of religion. By the early 20th century, the logical positivists attempted to set out criteria by which to distinguish genuinely objective forms of enquiry, which they limited to science and mathematics, from everything else, on the grounds that the claims of science were verifiable, whereas those of metaphysics and religion, for example, were not, and – since neither did they consist of 'analytic' truths like those of mathematics – they were meaningless. Although he was not a logical positivist as such, it was the philosopher Karl Popper who was taken to be most representative of this approach in the later 20th century. Popper substituted falsifiability for verifiability, and advanced the idea that the aim of scientific enquiry is not to try and confirm or verify one's theories, but to try to falsify them: this is the true form of intellectual honesty. Here, the 'scientist as hero' reaches his apogee, taking on the role of the ascetic by a form of intellectual self-deprivation. Fighting his natural inclinations, the scientist must himself try to show the theories he has nurtured to be false. In compensation, however, he attains to a form of intellectual morality of a profound kind to which no one else can reasonably aspire: the scientist becomes the only truly intellectually honest person, for only the scientist is so concerned for truth that he attempts to show that his own theories are false. Interestingly, Popper explicitly drew the connections between science and a democratic culture, so that objectivity became a general quality.

Objectivity and prior expectations

But is the kind of critical stance that Popper demands of science here possible? More specifically, is the falsification of theories such a straightforward procedure, or is it perhaps a piece of wishful thinking that fails to reflect how science actually proceeds? Since Popper is holding up scientific enquiry as a standard by which to judge all forms of enquiry, if his account of scientific practice is mistaken, there are important consequences for how we conceive objectivity more generally.

If we perform an experiment or carry out an observation, we usually have a good idea of what kind of result we will get. Sometimes we get unexpected results, and, when we are testing a theory, these results may contradict what the theory predicts the outcome should be. Shouldn't one reject the theory when this happens? After all, doesn't objectivity dictate that if a result of an experiment conflicts with our expectations then this shows that there is something wrong with our expectations? Certainly, Popper thought so, and this was the core idea behind his association of falsificationist methodology with intellectual honesty. But more recently, there has been a revival of the thesis of Pierre Duhem, a historian and philosopher of science working at the beginning of the last century, who argued that it is impossible to test any scientific hypothesis in isolation, because there are always auxiliary assumptions involved, and these are intimately tied in with the hypothesis itself. Even seemingly straightforward hypotheses are routinely part of a complex network. So when an observation or experiment yields a result that contradicts one's hypothesis, it could be one of the auxiliary hypotheses that is at fault, and not the one that the experiment was designed to test.

There are many examples of this, but perhaps the best known is Galileo's response to observations that seemed, unambiguously, to contradict the heliocentric theory. What is at issue here is his defence of the theory that it is the Earth that rotates daily on its axis, not the heavens that rotate around a stationary Earth. When Galileo proposed this theory, early in the 17th century, not one, but four pieces of evidence seemed to falsify it directly. First, if the Earth were rotating on its axis, then a body, such as a lead ball, dropped from the top of a tower, or one thrown vertically upwards, would not land directly at the bottom of the tower, or on the spot from which it was thrown, because in the time the body took to fall, the Earth would have moved. Consequently, we would expect it to land some distance from the original spot. But in fact it lands on the original spot. Second, if the Earth is rotating, bodies such as cannon balls which are fired in the direction of the Earth's rotation should have a smaller range than those fired in the opposite direction. But in fact they have the same range. Third, bodies that do not adhere to the Earth, such as clouds and birds, would not be able to keep up with the Earth's rotation. Fourth, potters' wheels demonstrate that bodies placed on a rapidly rotating surface are flung off that surface, yet we never experience the slightest lift, even in light bodies such as feathers, even at the Equator, where the speed of rotation is greatest (and very much faster than any potters' wheel).

These 'falsifications' of the theory of the Earth's diurnal rotation do not in fact mean that the Earth is stationary. What Galileo did was to reinterpret the evidence, successfully in the first three cases, unsuccessfully in the fourth. Take the first case. Proponents of the view that the ball would land away from the tower, Galileo tells us, find that confirmed by an experiment in which a rock is dropped from above onto a stationary boat, and then on to a moving boat. In the first case, the stone falls vertically downwards to the base of the mast, whereas in the second it falls into the water behind the boat, because in the time the ball has taken to fall, the boat has moved on. Galileo reconsiders what happens here in terms of two situations where a lead ball is dropped from the top of the mast of a moving ship. If we imagine the ship to be passing under a high bridge, in the first situation we hold the ball at the top of the mast and release it as soon as the ship has passed under the bridge. In the second situation, we imagine the ball to be suspended over the side of the bridge at exactly the height of the first ball so that as the ship emerges from the bridge and the two balls meet, they are released simultaneously. What actually happens, Galileo points out, is not that both fall some distance behind the ship: only the second ball does this, while the first falls directly to the base of the mast. In both cases, the ball is dropped from the same point, yet their behaviour during the fall is different. The reason for this, Galileo argues, is that the second ball starts from rest (relative to the situation described), so that when it is released, the only motion it has is vertically downwards. The first ball, by contrast, has been moving with the ship, and it does not suddenly lose the motion it shares with the ship when released. Consequently, the motion it undergoes during the fall is actually a resultant of two component motions: a horizontal motion in the same direction as the ship and a vertical motion downwards. We do not notice the horizontal motion because we take our bearings from the ship in this case, but if the ship suddenly disappeared, we would be alerted to this component of the motion.

On the face of it, this looks like a case of successfully ignoring considerations of objectivity in favour of reinterpreting the results to fit one's case. But this is only on the assumption that evidence is fixed in advance and requires no interpretation. Galileo's response is to reinterpret the evidence, arguing that what the observation shows is not the falsity of the hypothesis that the Earth moves, but the falsity of an implicit auxiliary hypothesis which his opponents hold: namely that the path of the falling body is not affected by whether it is initially in motion or stationary. Here, Galileo has a prior expectation, in that he believes that the Earth moves on independent astronomical grounds: for example, on the basis of his telescopic observations of the phases of Venus, which, as the heliocentric theory predicts, exhibits a full range of phases, like the Moon, whereas on the leading version of the geocentric theory, it should be permanently crescent-shaped. In other words, one set of observations supports the heliocentric theory, whereas another supports the geocentric theory, so it is a question of deciding which observation is the more reliable, where by 'observation' here we need to include its accompanying assumptions, which it is Galileo's genius to have uncovered and subjected to scrutiny.

In this case, then, the appearance of a violation of objectivity is just an appearance. We have a theory of how bodies should behave on the surface of a moving object, and a different theory that tells us that the Earth moves but that bodies on its surface do not behave in this way. The procedure of reinterpreting the former to remove the contradiction between the two is not a case of special pleading, and is not a sacrifice of objectivity. It is designed to show that one kind of procedure – telescopic observation – is reliable, whereas another – observation of the behaviour of falling bodies – is not reliable in itself and requires us to identify the prior condition of the falling body before we can draw any conclusions.

A slightly different kind of case can be illustrated by Arthur Eddington's 1919 empirical demonstration of the correctness of Einstein's general theory of relativity. This case is of significance because it has widely been regarded, including by Popper, as a 'crucial experiment', that is, one that provides clinching evidence for one theory over another. General relativity predicted that a gravitational field should bend rays of light more than was predicted by Newton's theory of gravity. The effect was slight, and required something of a great mass to be detectable. Einstein predicted that the Sun would deflect a ray of light by 1.75 seconds of an arc, a miniscule amount but twice the deflection predicted by Newtonian mechanics. He anticipated that the light from a distant star, whose position has been accurately fixed, would, when observed from the Earth, be deflected if it were blocked by the very edge of the Sun. The problem is that the Sun's brightness would prevent observation of such gravitational distortion. A solar eclipse, where the effect of the Sun's brightness is briefly removed, would create an opportunity for observation, however. Eddington, the greatest astronomical observer of his age, travelled to the island of Principe, off the coast of Africa, to achieve ideal viewing conditions for a predicted eclipse. On the basis of the photographs he was able to take, he announced that the Sun had caused a deflection of 1.61 minutes of an arc, compared with photographs taken when the Sun was not present.

If anything could count as a crucial experiment, this should, but there were complications. Eddington was convinced of the truth of general relativity on theoretical grounds, but the theory faced very significant opposition from his English scientific colleagues. The result he got was the one he expected, but in reality it was not a crucial experiment. It is far from clear that the margin of error in his observations was in fact adequate, and subsequent controversy arose over whether his equipment was sufficiently accurate to yield the precision required to compare the predictions of the two theories. Moreover, Eddington discounted simultaneous observations at Sobral in Brazil, which appeared closer to the Newtonian model, but most astronomers subsequently accepted that there was a fault in the telescopes used for these observations. His own observations were extremely good by contemporary standards, and there were no better observations made that undermined his result. They were not perfect, but very reliable results. Moreover, the case bears some similarity to that of Galileo on the paths of falling bodies, in that there were good independent theoretical grounds for believing that general relativity gave a better account than Newtonian mechanics. In short, if we remember that objectivity is a matter of degree, not an absolute notion, and that what we want out of astronomical observations is that they follow the most reliable procedures, then Eddington's stand up well in terms of objectivity.

Finally, what about cases where there are problems arising from prior expectations but no good independent theoretical grounds supporting those expectations? Examples arise especially where the outcome is generated by statistical sampling, in which case the results are yielded not just by the statistical procedures used but also by the assumptions behind the classificatory categories used, as well as by the questions asked.

A good example is IQ (intelligence quotient) testing. In 1994, a spirited defence of the IQ test results, including the differential results for racial groups, appeared in Richard Herrnstein's and Charles Murray's *The Bell Curve*. The claim was that there is an accurate measure of intelligence (which the authors, albeit with qualifications, treat as inherited), that it is distributed as a bell-shaped curve – what mathematicians call a Gaussian distribution – and that extensive surveys indicate that American blacks score significantly worse than American whites. In the course of a review of the book, the philosopher Ian Hacking notes that the first extensive IQ tests were performed on US army recruits in 1917, and African Americans did worse than whites. This was evidently expected, so the results met the testers' expectations. But when the tests were subsequently performed on the population in general, women had higher scores than men. This didn't seem right to the testers, so they identified the questions that the women did better on and replaced them. As a result, women and men came out equal. This was not the end of the matter however. A month after the appearance of Hacking's review, a letter appeared in the same journal recounting a similar experience in Kenya in 1930. A psychologist, R. A. C. Oliver, had been employed by a major US corporation to seek out talented blacks who could subsequently be sent to college and trained as teachers. Oliver used an IQ test to do this, experimenting with what was considered the most reliable form of nonverbal testing, the Porteus Maze Test. The local blacks, it turned out, approached maze problems in a very different way from the white children for whom the test had originally been devised, and scored higher, demonstrating maze-solving techniques and skills that were beyond those of the white population. The questions were removed from subsequent IQ tests.

In these cases, the response to countervailing evidence is dictated by prior expectations. What is wrong with this? We saw that Galileo reinterpreted evidence, to good effect. Is essentially the same kind of thing happening here? The cases are surely very different. Galileo had a choice between two sets of results, one of which he had reason to believe was scientifically reliable, the other which made very common but questionable assumptions. In the IQ case, the expectations are not shaped by reliable scientific theories which clash with the unexpected results. Present-day IQ tests make sure to include questions that balance verbal skills against spatial skills, for example, as men and women perform differently on these questions, and it is evidently assumed that such differences do not reflect differences in intelligence. But they do not include the kinds of differences in maze-solving that whites do comparatively poorly on as an indication of intelligence. IQ tests can no more show that blacks are not as intelligent as whites than they can show that males and females are equally intelligent. Only prior expectations could lead to such assessments.

It would, nevertheless, be a mistake to conclude that the procedures that the devisors of the tests have had to adopt, to keep the results within their range of expectations, wholly disqualify

IQ testing. If we think of the tests in terms not of intelligence but of the suitability for achieving particular educational goals, they may have some value when combined with other forms of assessment. Such tests may complement examinations which rely on memory, for example. It may also be the case that educationalists are able to use the bottom end of the IQ spectrum to identify those likely to benefit from remedial education. On the other hand, what the problems of expectation-driven testing do clearly call into question is the reliability of IQ tests as a method that would identify any presumed racial and gender variations in intelligence.

We started our discussion in this chapter with the question of the relation between objectivity and intellectual honesty, and we have pursued this via the question of the relation between our theories and evidence. This relation is not straightforward, as the problem of prior expectations reveals, for sometimes prior expectations may play a legitimate role, whereas sometimes they do not. Comparing theories and evidence is certainly a matter which impinges on objectivity, and there are objective and non-objective ways of dealing with evidence. But Popper's attempt to argue that scientific procedure is the standard of objectivity works on the assumption that in science, by contrast with other forms of enquiry, it is a straightforward matter of comparing one's theories with the evidence. Wishful idealizations about how science proceeds cannot form the basis for an understanding of objectivity.

Chapter 3

Doesn't science show there is no objectivity?

In the last chapter, we saw that the relation between scientific theories and evidence can be complex, and provides no straightforward criterion by which to judge objectivity. But to say that objectivity in science is not a simple matter, and that this should put us on our guard against extrapolating from science, is of course not to say that there is no objectivity in science. Yet two developments in science in the 20th century have sometimes been thought to undermine the notion of objectivity completely. It is often thought that a relativity of observation to the investigators' beliefs or theories or values or location is demonstrated by two cases in 20th-century physics, relativity theory and quantum mechanics, on the grounds that these provide examples of the way in which observational results depend on the observer. Relativity theory has been interpreted as showing that observations are physically relative to the observer, in that space, time, and motion are all relative. Developments in quantum mechanics have been taken to show that observation always physically affects the thing observed and interacts with it, so that we can never measure the object as it is in its own right. A similar interactionist view is found in a number of social science disciplines, which add the qualification that all observations inevitably involve a degree of cultural relativity in the observer.

Does relativity theory show that everything is relative?

In his special theory of relativity, the account of which was published in 1905, Albert Einstein explained the behaviour of moving bodies in a new way, one which introduced a degree of relativity into space, time, and motion. Before the 17th century, rest and motion were considered absolute, both in the sense that the universe could be divided up into definite locations or places, by reference to which one could be said to be either at rest or in motion, and in the sense that one would always be able to tell whether one was moving or not. This view was rejected in the 17th century, and Galileo argued that rest and uniform motion in a straight line were indistinguishable. To give a modern example, if one is sitting in a train carriage, looking out of the window, and an adjacent train crosses one's field of vision, it can be impossible to tell whether one's own train is moving, say, north at 5 kilometers an hour, or the other train is moving south at 5 kilometers an hour. There is an equivalence of rest and uniform motion in a straight line. We can say that our train has a velocity of 5 miles an hour in a northerly direction and the other a velocity of 0 kilometers an hour, or vice versa. Alternatively, we can say that our train has a velocity of 4 miles an hour in a northerly direction and the other a velocity of 1 kilometer an hour in a southerly direction. Or that our train has a velocity of 10 miles an hour in a northerly direction and the other a velocity of 5 kilometers an hour in a northerly direction. The motion we experience is the difference between the two, and it is a relative motion. We can even say that, when the train is moving relative to the Earth, the motion can just as easily be described as being that of the Earth, in the other direction. It is simply a question of subtracting one velocity from the other.

Classical mechanics, essentially that of Galileo and Newton, stipulated that motions and velocities were relative. In one sense, Einstein's theory of special relativity removes a degree of relativity, because it denies that velocities are relative in this sense, namely, that the velocity of a body is simply a question of subtracting one velocity from another. The reasoning behind this is best illustrated by Einstein's reaction to a famous experiment performed in 1887 to measure the speed of light, named after the experimenters, Michelson and Morley. Michelson and Morley measured the speed of light from the Sun first from a point on the surface of the Earth rotating away from the Sun, and then from a point on the Earth rotating towards the Sun. The first measured speed should be less than the second in the same way that the relative speed of a car overtaking one's own is less than that of a car coming in the opposite direction. But Michelson and Morley discovered that the speed of light is the same whether one is moving towards its source or away from it. Einstein argued, in response, that the speed of light is absolute, not relative, and that the procedure of adding or subtracting velocities does not hold strictly even at everyday velocities, though in the latter case the effect is so slight as to be undetectable.

On the special theory of relativity, the speed of light is the same for all observers, regardless of their motion, whereas space and time dilate and contract depending on the speed of the body from which they are measured. If a body is moving towards you, it is measured as being shortened, for example. The same kind of phenomenon occurs in respect to time: moving clocks are measured as ticking more slowly. Not only are space and time affected in their own right by the revisions that Einstein introduces, but because these are relativized to frames, so is the phenomenon of simultaneity. Two events may be simultaneous for one observer yet not be for another who is in motion relative to the first observer, and in that case there is no right answer to the question whether the events are really simultaneous.

In short, the space and time in terms of which we measure the speeds of things are themselves affected by the speeds of things, and there is no absolute frame by which observers can agree, for example, on phenomena such as whether spatially separated events have occurred simultaneously. Special relativity certainly makes particular phenomena relative which were not relative before – measures of space, measures of time, and simultaneity – but it makes the speed of light in a vacuum the same for all observers, irrespective of their relative velocities. In other words, it changes what is relative and what is fixed: it does not simply make everything relative.

The physical theory of relativity has no consequences for our understanding of objectivity. It tells us that, whereas we previously thought that whether two events occur simultaneously was an absolute matter, it turns out to be relative. But special relativity is an objective theory of the phenomena. The content of the theory is not affected by any of the physical phenomena that it describes. It is not as if its truth is relative to some physical state.

The interaction of observers and the observed

The theory of relativity does not undermine objectivity in science, but on the face of it quantum mechanics presents something of a challenge in this respect. There are, however, in reality two separate issues as far as quantum mechanics is concerned.

The first is that, because of the ways in which certain properties are connected at the microscopic level, one cannot measure certain pairs of properties at the same time: a precise measurement of position and a precise measurement of momentum is not possible. The more precise the first measurement, the less precise the second, and vice versa. One of the problems in the early development of quantum mechanics was accounting for how electrons jumped from one orbit to another, and this was solved in part by Heisenberg's 'matrix mechanics', which allowed one to calculate the probability of an electron jumping from one orbit to another. Matrix mechanics enables one to represent position and momentum in arrays of numbers called matrices. If position and momentum matrices are both applied to a state, however, then the result we get differs depending on which we apply first, because the way in which the mathematics works means that operations performed on the matrices are non-commutative, that is, the quantities cannot be transposed: a × b does not equal b × a. The upshot of this is that it is impossible to know both quantities simultaneously with the same degree of precision.

This is closely associated with, but not quite the same as, the second issue, which is that the act of measuring physically interferes with the measured object. One early interpretation of this phenomenon, the Copenhagen Interpretation, formulated by the physicists Niels Bohr, Werner Heisenberg, and others in the years 1924 to 1927, maintained that particles were not in a physical state when not being measured: it was the act of measurement, which involved an interaction between a measuring apparatus and a measured system, that put them in a physical state. Moreover, on the Copenhagen Interpretation, this interaction is very problematic and peculiar because the measuring system obeys classical laws, whereas the measured system obeys quantum laws.

The lesson that some have drawn from this is that measurement or observation affects the system observed, so we can never know what the system would be like without observation or measurement. The peculiarities of quantum mechanics make it difficult to understand even in its own right, and in fact what seems to have happened is not that people have studied quantum mechanics carefully and have tried to draw consequences from it, but rather have not studied it at all. Quantum mechanics itself has no consequences for the general question of objectivity. However, if one takes the second issue that I have isolated – interference – as what is at stake, ignoring the first, then one can indeed raise the general question of objectivity. This is what has happened. The question of the impossibility of accurately measuring both momentum and position has simply been assimilated to the issue of interference, which is something that has a much longer history than quantum mechanics. What is in effect claimed is that there is an analogy between the quantum mechanics case and one that may arise in the observation of human behaviour, for example, where the fact of being observed might inevitably and perhaps unconsciously lead one to modify one's behaviour.

The analogy breaks down, however. The problem in quantum mechanics is that position and momentum in micro-particles don't have a physically determinate value in themselves. There is no analogue to this in history, law, and the other disciplines. But more importantly for our purposes, the case of modification of behaviour is something which we can develop techniques for dealing with, whereas this is explicitly not possible in the Copenhagen interpretation of quantum mechanics. Such techniques have been around since antiquity, and were further developed in the 16th century in the context of legal and historical testimony in a particularly interesting way. Francesco Patrizzi, in his *Dialogues on History* of 1560, had attempted to show that the historian can either be impartial, or informed, but not both. He begins by rejecting secondary sources as virtual hearsay, and he divides primary sources into the partisan and the objective. Then, replying on a number of Machiavellian assumptions about the nature of rulers, he sets up a dichotomy between the partisan observer and the objective observer. Partisan observers – in this case, those sympathetic to the ruler – in virtue of being partisan, have access to the relevant information, because the ruler can rely upon them, but because they are partisan they will not provide an objective account of this information. By contrast, objective observers, namely those who are prepared to be critical of the ruler if this is merited, will not have the ruler's confidence (precisely because they are objective), and so will not have access to the source of the relevant information. The example is not a far-fetched one: consider only the very widespread practice of government briefings to selected journalists.

Patrizzi concluded that it is 'utterly and totally impossible for human actions to be known as they were actually done.' His contemporaries responded that there are a number of ways in which we can establish credibility and plausibility, similar to those applied in law where, for example, doubts are held about a witness's credibility, and we take into account such factors as the probative value of corroborative testimonies. In short, the problem is not one of a sceptical challenge to the objectivity of history *per se* but rather problems about evidence and reliability. Practitioners of the discipline will usually be best placed to deal with these. The same range of solutions is available to the anthropologist or psychologist, for example, who is concerned that the observation of his or her subjects causes them to modify their behaviour or statements in some way.

In short, the quantum mechanics case is different from that of the changes that interference can induce in measurement and observation. The fact that something or someone may alter its behaviour when being measured or observed, does not in itself mean that objectivity is not possible. All it means is that new procedures have to be devised to secure objectivity.

Chapter 4

Isn't all perception and understanding relative?

Many of the philosophical arguments that have come down to us from the first Greek philosophers turn on the question of whether we can know things as they really are, or whether all knowledge is relative to us. The thrust of these arguments, in the more sophisticated form they attained in the work of the philosopher Aenesidemus in the 1st century BCE, was that perception was always relative to the observer, the conditions under which the observation was made, and the state the object was in when it was perceived. He argued that one could not remove any of these, and ask how things were in their own right. These arguments rely not merely on the observer's state of mind, but more importantly on physical characteristics of the observer and the observer's environment, and on the interaction between the observer and the environment. They deny that objectivity is possible, in the sense that they maintain that any experience of the world necessarily involves contingent or idiosyncratic conditions of perception and understanding. We need to ask whether this is the case, and if so, whether it would render objectivity unachievable.

Traditional scepticism

The traditional arguments for relativism start from the premise that things appear different to different people depending on a variety of circumstances, and that any attempt to decide between these different appearances depends on our having a criterion by which to judge them, which prompts the question where such a criterion could come from.

Consider the case of sense perception. There is manifestly a connection between how we perceive the world and what kind of sense organs we have. Aenesidemus pointed out that things must appear differently to animals with different sensory anatomies, for example. Some species of animals have eyes that are more convex and more set into the body than others, and so will see things differently from animals of a different species, who may have eyes on stalks, for example. Some animals have feathers, some scales, some spikes, some flesh, and so their sense of touch will differ from one another. We have no criterion by which to decide between these. There is simply no way in which things *really* feel: it depends on whether one has skin, or spikes, or fur. Similarly with vision. There is no way in which things *really* look: they just look one way to those with eyes of a certain kind, and another way to those with eyes of a different kind. In particular, we cannot say that how the world appears to animals with bulging eyes is not veridical on the grounds that we can check our visual image of the world against touch. That is, we cannot use the fact that we can feel that what we see as a smooth surface is smooth, and can feel that what we see as a curved surface is in fact curved, to demonstrate that how the world looks to an animal with bulging eyes does not correspond to how it really is. This won't work, for it assumes that variations in visual organs can be matched against unvarying tactile information. But we not only have visual organs of a particular type, we also have tactile organs of a particular type. An animal with bulging eyes and spikes on its tactile organs, with nerves in the tactile organ that detect pressure quite differently from human sense organs, for example, could conceivably have a match between its visual and tactile images, even though these are different from ours.

Consider the difference between vultures' eyes and human eyes on perception of shape. For vision (as opposed to simple sensitivity to light) to occur, we need a lens, a piece of transparent material with a curved surface, which refracts incoming light rays so that they come to a single focus. Human eyes have uniform curvature. Vultures' eyes, by contrast, have a greater curvature in the centre than in the periphery of the lens, resulting in greater magnification in the centre, which allows them to spot potential prey with greater acuity. If we look at an ordinary bar, we see two parallel lines, whereas the lens in the vulture's eye presents an image with a bulge in the middle. The natural reaction to this difference is to say that the vulture's lens introduces a distortion, but what makes the vulture's image less objective than ours? We cannot test this by comparing the two images with that produced by a flat glass slide, for example, because a flat piece of glass is not a lens. Curvature is necessary for vision, and it is hard to see on what legitimate grounds uniform curvature could be preferred – in the sense of providing a veridical image – over non-uniform curvature. I say 'legitimate' because we cannot, for example, smuggle in any assumptions about a flat refracting surface being the norm, thinking that uniform curvature deviates from such a supposed norm less than does non-uniform curvature. That would be to misunderstand the nature of vision. Can we instead compare the two visual images with the shape that we feel when we run our fingers along the bar? The problem with this is that one might argue, from the perspective of vultures' eyes, that this is how parallel surfaces feel when they move from the periphery of one's visual field to its centre. After all, we in effect make a similar claim with human vision in the case of parallel lines, which appear to converge the more distant they are.

Is the choice between saying that the world just is as human sense organs present it, on the one hand, and, on the other, saying that what shape things are and what their colour is are completely relative?

We should resist being forced into embracing either of these alternatives. One thing that seems reasonably clear from the examples of colour and shape is that there can be legitimate dispute about what is relative and what is absolute, and that, upon reflection, we may decide in particular cases that something which we had considered to be absolute turns out to be relative. The question is whether reflection on such particular cases could lead us to conclude that we may be mistaken in the general case: that *everything* we thought to be absolute turns out to be relative. Aenesidemus thought it could. He maintained that *everything* is relative to the observer and to the conditions of observation, and there can never be an issue of right and wrong here.

This kind of argument works with two strategies. First, there is a move from cases where it is agreed that we cannot establish objectivity to the claim that all cases turn out to be like these. Second, all assumptions and values are assimilated to prejudice or bias, and it is then argued that there can be no account of the world that doesn't involve some assumptions and values, and hence prejudice or bias, and therefore there can be no objective account of the world.

The first argument effectively works on the assumption that there is a continuum between cases where subjective elements are evident and those where they are present but not evident. The move from the one to the other is helped along by substituting relative versions of properties for absolute ones. For example, Aenesidemus argues that how things appear to us depends on our position, giving the example of a boat which appears small when far away but large when close. Is the size of the boat as it is when seen from far away, or from close by? Any choice, he points out, would be arbitrary, so we are unable to establish any criterion by which to decide. The claim is that there is no objective fact of the matter: the ship is neither *really* small nor *really* large. But there is a sleight of hand here. The ship has, of course, definite dimensions, which are objective: they can be measured and checked by anyone. What has happened is that this way of presenting the dimensions of the ship, which is independent of where we are standing in relation to the ship, has been translated into a different form of description, one which – instead of working in terms of absolute sizes, in metres, for example – works in terms of relative sizes, namely large and small. Of course, in measuring the length of something we need to place the measuring instrument next to the object measured. We cannot measure it (directly) if we are standing several feet away from it. To give it a determinate size, we need to observe certain non-arbitrary rules about positioning, the markings on the measuring instrument, and so on. In the case of relative sizes, there are no such rules. This is the crucial difference, and what makes it illegitimate to move from one to the other. One can often describe properties such as distance, temperature, size, and weight both in absolute and in relative terms. But this in itself does not undermine the objective properties. Even if everything that had an absolute description also had a relative one, this would manifestly not entail that everything was thereby relative.

The second strategy in the repertoire of relativism is a little more serious, for it is also unwittingly adopted by some defenders of objectivity. It involves a conflation of assumptions and values, on the one hand, and prejudice or bias, on the other. Everyone agrees that a judgement cannot be objective if it carries prejudice or bias, so clearly if all assumptions and values can be assimilated to prejudice or bias, and if it can be shown that there can be no account of the world that doesn't involve some assumptions and values, then there can be no objective account of the world. Now there is no doubt that there is a grey area between assumptions and prejudices. However, grey areas do not invalidate distinctions: there is a clear distinction between someone having a full head of hair and someone being bald, despite the fact that there are cases where it is not clear which category a person with thinning hair comes in. We cannot perceive or think without assumptions of various kinds, but the fact that there is a grey area between reasonable assumptions and prejudice does not mean that we cannot think without prejudices.

The deeper issues here go beyond the arguments used to establish relativism. We must also examine the picture, to which such arguments are implicitly committed, of what true objectivity would look like, were we able to achieve it. The argument moves from the idea that we remove all bias from our theories to removing all preconceptions from them. But since this latter is impossible, it is claimed that objectivity thereby becomes impossible. To respond to this, we must ask: if objectivity does not consist in stripping our ideas back to the basics, what does it consist in? Could it be that objective ideas are richer, rather than poorer: that they have more content, as opposed to less content? Consider Aenesidemus' argument concerning the colour of gold. We cannot ask what colour gold is, he argues, because the colour of a substance varies depending on what state it is in (gold is yellow when it is solid and white in powder form), what state the observer is in (whether, for example, the observer has jaundice), and what the intervening medium is (whether the substance is viewed in air or in water, through coloured transparent material, and so on). But as far as objectivity is concerned, what we seek here is not some means by which to identify which of these states corresponds to reality. Aenesidemus' argument sets out to establish that, as far as the colour of gold is concerned, there is no truth of the matter. But what we are looking for from an objective theory is not something that will lead us to establish the *real* colour of gold, but rather something that can predict how a powder will look when viewed through different coloured glasses, for example, how something will look if we have jaundice, and perhaps even predict colour changes when a solid is ground into a powder. An objective theory is not one that simply chooses one set of viewing conditions over others and then stipulates that these will be the objective conditions.

It is not a 'view from nowhere', in philosophers' jargon. It does not tell us that, if we remove all viewing conditions, that is what the object will be like. Rather, it tells us how it will look under any conditions, ideally, or failing that how it will look in a specified range of conditions. In seeking to be objective, we are seeking interpretations and judgements that hold up against all alternatives when judged by the same criteria. Any perceptual judgement involves, as well as input from the object perceived, various inputs from our perceptual and cognitive faculties, and we might reasonably expect this latter type of input to take on an increasingly significant role as we move away from straightforward observation, and as questions of objectivity become potentially more pressing. What we see and what we judge are dependent on various perceptual-cum-cognitive interpretations that we place on our observations. And, of course, the conceptual structuring and interpretation might have been different: we might have evolved differently, for example if humans had found themselves in a completely different physical environment. This does not rob our observations of objectivity. Objectivity is a feature of judgements that we make about the world, and judgements involve concepts and theories. To think otherwise is to assume that objectivity can be secured only in the absence of interpretation and judgement, but in fact the question of objectivity does not even arise in the absence of these. Objectivity only becomes an issue when we raise the question of the standing of our judgements and interpretations.

Chapter 5
What about our conceptual structuring of the world?

We don't just see things: we see them in a particular way, as particular things. Our sensory systems and our minds interact with the world to produce representations of it. How does this bear on the question of objectivity? There are three cases that we can distinguish. The first simply rests on the idea that we structure the world in perception. Although we all do it in the same way, nevertheless we all bring something to our perceptions, and the question is whether what we bring to perception undermines its objectivity. The second is the claim that different cultural and linguistic groups structure the world differently. Here the possibility is raised that there are different 'ways of seeing the world', each legitimate in its own right. The third case moves from perceptual structuring to a theoretical account of the world, of the kind offered in the various sciences, where we order our conceptions of the world in various ways in an effort to understand it, but where these orderings may differ and be in competition with one another. Here the question of whether we can make an objective choice between these arises.

Conceptual structuring

The publication of Immanuel Kant's *Critique of Pure Reason* in 1781 inaugurated a new era in philosophy, one dominated by the question of what contribution the mind made to our experience of the world: how it shaped what we experience. Kant argued that this contribution is far greater than had been imagined up to this point, and that the world that we grasp in perception and in thought is in effect constructed by the mind. Moreover, on Kant's account, we can have no knowledge of the world as it is in itself, for such knowledge requires us to access the world in some way, but the means of access always shape what we experience and know. We don't have to accept Kant's conclusion here to appreciate that we need to investigate the means by which we access the world before we can make judgements about any correspondence between our mental representation of the world and the world itself. Moreover, the idea that all experience and thought involves conceptual structuring clearly bears on the question of how objective our theories about the world are, for such structuring is not something over which we have any control, and is not open to rational assessment or revision.

To get a sense of Kant's argument, take the examples of space and time. Are these part of the world, or part of our conceptual structuring of the world? Kant reflected upon the idea that we can imagine a universe without motion, a universe in which bodies are stationary. He also reflected on the fact that we can imagine a universe without matter in it, for example by imagining a universe in which the matter is gradually removed so there is none left. But, he noted, we can't imagine a universe without space and time. We can't think of a universe empty of matter and mentally remove space from it, because we simply cannot imagine a universe becoming spaceless. Now one thing this might mean is that space and time exist in a way that is more fundamental than matter. There could not be a universe without space and time, but there could be one without matter. Moreover, matter requires space and time for its existence, so somehow space and time are more basic than matter: they are, as philosophers would put it, ontologically prior to matter. But Kant's approach is different. The question is not one of metaphysics – what the constituents of the world are – but one of epistemology, what our access to the world is. He says that if we cannot even imagine a universe without space and time, this tells us something about us, not something about the universe. What it shows, he argues, is that we cannot think about physical events without thinking about them spatio-temporally, and this is a feature of our ability to think about physical events, not a feature of physical events themselves. The same considerations, he argues, hold for causality. Space, time, and causation are conditions of possibility of our being able to think about, perceive, and have beliefs about physical events in the first place.

On this view, the world is not differentiated into separate things in its own right. Rather, it resembles an undifferentiated continuum, upon which the basic categories of thought impose structure so that the continuum can be carved up into discrete things and properties. This carving up is an involuntary and unchangeable feature of how we experience the world, not something over which we have any control, rational or otherwise. The question here, however, is not whether this means that our experience of the world cannot be objective, but rather whether we should be thinking in terms of objectivity in the first place. If what we are talking about is a fixed and unchanging feature of experience in general, then this is something about which we can neither exercise objectivity nor fail to exercise objectivity. Of course, we may reject Kant's picture of space, time, and causation as being preconditions of experience rather than autonomous contents of experience, but in doing so we are not questioning his account on the grounds of lack of objectivity.

Cognitive and linguistic relativity

If we conceive of conceptual structuring as a universal feature of the mind, then there is no threat to objectivity, because questions of objectivity simply cannot arise. Sense organs and the brain do not just register the world. Our minds structure our experience and our thought in fundamental ways. To think that this in itself could compromise objectivity is to imagine that we could think without brains, see without eyes. To the extent to which this is Kant's point about our perceiving the world only as phenomenal (as it is structured by our minds) and not as it is in itself (as it is in its unstructured form), then this is just to say that we cannot think without minds any more than we can see without eyes. Unmediated perception (and thought) is not objective perception: it is not perception at all. As such, it cannot provide a model of objectivity to which we can aspire. However, once we move from the idea that conceptual structuring is a universal feature of the mind, to the view that this structuring varies in some way, for example from culture to culture or from language to language, it seems that objectivity faces a challenge, for the world now seems to be whatever we believe it to be, and these beliefs vary depending on a host of contingent cultural and linguistic factors.

In the late 18th century, there arose an attempt to understand human behaviour not in religious terms, or in terms of morals or political philosophy, but in terms of what subsequently developed as anthropology. The interests of late 18th-century and early 19th-century writers such as Johann Gottfried Herder and Wilhelm von Humboldt lay in history, philosophy, and that branch of linguistics known as philology. Different language groups, they argued, embody and express different cultural and cognitive traits. It is not just a question of linguistic differences: these linguistic differences encode different ways of thinking about and seeing the world. Humboldt's view was that Indo-European languages were naturally superior to those of other families, but when the linguistic relativity thesis was taken up again at the end of the 19th century, this was rejected in favour of an equality of all languages. The anthropologist Franz Boas argued that ethnographers studying other cultures could not engage in such study properly without first learning the language. Boas's student Edward Sapir offered the classic version of the linguistic relativity doctrine when he announced that 'no two languages are ever sufficiently similar to be considered as representing the same social reality. The worlds in which different societies live are distinct worlds, not merely the same world with different labels attached.' The consequences of this were explored further in the work of his student Benjamin Lee Whorf, in what became known as the Sapir–Whorf thesis.

The Sapir–Whorf thesis holds that we impose structure on nature in terms of categories supplied largely by our language. The world presents itself to us as a flux of impressions which have little coherence in their own right. It is the task of the mind to organize these impressions into discrete ingredients, connect these by way of concepts, and ascribe significance to various parts of the world as perceived. What regulates this process, Whorf argued, was not some identifiable physical evidence which constrained us to come to particular conclusions about the world, but rather our similar conceptual understanding, which is dictated by our shared language. Without this shared language, we can expect very significant differences. Whorf advances a number of examples of what he claims are radical differences between European and indigenous North American languages. In the Hopi language, water, for example, is represented in a variety of ways which do not correspond to our usage. Similarly, Whorf claims, there are many words for snow in Inuit languages which are not capturable in other languages. Even more fundamentally, investigating the language and culture of the Hopi, he argues that even a fundamental category like time is variable. This is a particularly interesting case, because, as we have seen, it was one of the basic forms of structuring that Kant argued was a universal feature of the mind. Whorf's argument was that the Hopi treated time as a continuous flow, and had no words for discrete intervals like days of the week, or hours of the day.

There are two main problems with the view that different cultures and languages carve up the world differently. First, carving things up in different ways doesn't necessarily have relativist consequences. Second, those who put a relativist interpretation on it tend to think of the carving up as the work of a single coordinated faculty, whereas in fact this is not the case.

On the first question, defenders of the Sapir–Whorf thesis often point, for example, to the fine-grained nature of the vocabulary for snow in Inuit languages, and the variations in colour terminology and classification in different languages, as evidence of the ways in which languages and cultures cut across one another in their classification of the world. But the fact that languages and cultures have different words for things, and have fine discriminations lacking in or cutting across those in other languages, in itself harbours no relativistic consequences. English nomenclature in organic chemistry (the drug LSD, for example, is (6aR,9R)-N, N-diethyl-7-methyl-4,6,6a,7,8,9-hexahydroindolo-[4,3-fg] quinoline-9-carboxamide) is far more fine-grained than anything to be found in the varieties of snow or water identified in Inuit languages. Moreover, this nomenclature cuts across many common distinctions while at the same time co-existing unproblematically with common usage. Similarly, there may be a shift from one understanding of a fundamental concept to another within a single culture without any relativistic consequences following.

Consider the measurement of time. Medieval and early modern communities measured time in a very different way from ours. The standard units of time that they employed varied in size from season to season. The day was divided into twelve sections on a sundial, for example, but since the length of the day varied from mid-summer to mid-winter, the length of the units varied: winter hours were much shorter than summer hours. In the context of allocating time for work in an agrarian subsistence economy, it is surely odd to say that the modern conception is more objective than the earlier one. The modern conception, which allows for precision in the measurements of time, such as those needed in the construction of clocks for calculating longitude, is simply suited to different purposes than the earlier conception. It is designed to do something different, and indeed the two conceptions can coexist. Modern (analogue) clockfaces, for example, while they enable us to tell hours and minutes, can only be read by someone trained to read the time, because clocks were originally designed to tell the hour, and the numerals on their faces only designate hours, not minutes: so 1:45, for example, is represented by a hand on 1 and a hand on 9.

If different conceptual schemes are at play in the examples adduced by advocates of the Sapir–Whorf thesis, they are quite compatible with one another, and harbour no relativist consequences. They are doing different things, serving different purposes.

On the second point, the Sapir–Whorf thesis works on the assumption of holism, that is, that the ways of carving up the world cohere and come as part of a package. This is crucial to the core thesis that what one believes shapes what one sees as much as does the thing seen. It is a matter of imposing a single structure on an undifferentiated continuum. But this is not how the brain works. Many of its functions are modularized. Modularization is an evolutionary response to increase in brain size, where increase in the number of neural pathways has to be balanced against the decrease in neural connectivity due to greater separation between nerve cells, which means it takes more time for signals to travel between cells. Primates, in particular, have evolved so as to segregate like-functioned neurones into highly connected modules, which have fewer long-distance connections: segregation of right and left hemispheres is just the largest and most obvious form of modularization of neural organization.

Modularity is manifested in human perception in a number of ways, not least in cases such as the Müller-Lyer illusion, where, in the illustration, the upper line looks shorter than the lower one, even though they are of the same length:

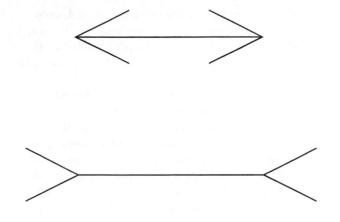

The interesting thing about this illusion is that knowing that it is an illusion – for example, as a result of taking a ruler to the figures and measuring each of the lines – doesn't affect our perception of the lines as being of different length. How we see them is quarantined off from our beliefs and from other similarly autonomously functioning modules. We do not know just how extensive modularization is in us. Some philosophers have suggested that modularity is rampant, and that it can account for our ability to hold contradictory views at the same time. But rampant or not, it shows that there are a number of cases where our beliefs do not, and cannot, shape what we see.

The Structure of Scientific Revolutions

We have seen that there can be different conceptual schemes which are quite compatible with one another, because they are serving different purposes. The problems arise when what is at issue is not carving up the world differently for different purposes, but alternative and competing ways of carving up the same world. The best examples here come from the history of science, in particular from the approach advocated in Thomas Kuhn's *The Structure of Scientific Revolutions* (1962) and the works that followed in its wake.

The Structure of Scientific Revolutions was not just philosophy of science, or history of science, or sociology of science. It was all three, with the addition of what might be called 'psychology of science' as a catalyst. Kuhn argued that major changes in scientific thinking – scientific revolutions – did not merely involve the rejection of one theory and its replacement by another, but a wholesale replacement of one worldview by another incommensurable worldview. The driving force behind the argument was a conception of science as consisting of conceptual schemes – the main ingredient in what Kuhn calls 'paradigms' – which determine how we see the world, and which vary not with cultural or linguistic differences but with differences in scientific theories. Because of the intimate way in which these conceptual structures and scientific theories are tied together, considerations that might be thought distinctive of shifts in conceptual structures – where a change in beliefs that alters how we see the world does not have to be motivated rationally or empirically – come to be associated with changes of scientific theory. In this way, it appears that objectivity is under threat.

Before the appearance of *The Structure of Scientific Revolutions*, the dominant account of the development of science supported a very strong and unqualified form of objectivity for science. The account had two mutually reinforcing components. The first was that scientific theories develop in a cumulative way. The story is one of constant improvement, as science gradually builds up results, correcting earlier theories and replacing them with new ones. The idea behind this is that the aim of science has always been the same, namely to mirror reality, and what matters is not so much where one starts from as the direction one is going in. This is where the second ingredient comes in, namely the idea that the history of science is unidirectional, and any account of it is essentially a form of genealogy, that is, a tracing of contemporary science back to its roots. The aim was to explain how we got to where we are now, which meant that the only context within which scientific theories – whether of remote antiquity or of the modern period – could be discussed was that of the present. This conception of the history of science, whereby it was a matter of shedding false theories and adopting true ones in a continuous development, was often accompanied by an account of the obstacles to this development, and here religion figured very prominently as the chief source of prejudices holding science back. What was identified as the characteristic feature of the road to truth was adherence to a scientific method. This is what the pioneers of the 17th-century scientific revolution had identified as what was wrong with the work of their Aristotelian predecessors: not lack of empirical information, or lack of ingenuity in dealing with it, but an approach to empirical matters which was wholly misguided.

Before the 18th and 19th centuries, discussions of scientific method were very much a matter of attempting to offer guidance in specific areas of research, and when the guidance took a more general form, it was still practical in orientation: how to avoid dead ends, what to do first in exploring a new area, how to educate oneself in a new area. In the course of the 18th and 19th centuries, however, the nature of discussions of scientific method changed from something essentially exploratory to something essentially didactic. In the 19th century, in particular, scientific method now comprised drawing methodological lessons from a successful model of scientific practice, typically identified with Newton's works. By contrast with earlier times, the guiding idea turned on examples of theories that embodied success, so the goal was to extract the active ingredient, as it were, from this model. However, there was never agreement on what exactly this scientific method was.

The Structure of Scientific Revolutions broke with the assumptions underlying theories of scientific method. It abandoned the notion that scientific progress was cumulative, at the same time rejecting the idea that explaining how we got to where we are now was what understanding the development of science consisted in. What is at issue in the Kuhnian account is not the idea of prejudices and biases as an obstacle to scientific development, but the consequences of treating scientific theories in terms of conceptual structures for our understanding of objectivity. These conceptual structures, which Kuhn terms 'paradigms', determine or constrain what intellectual options are available and what strategies are likely to be promising. Paradigms fix the appropriate terminology, guide the interpretation of experiments, and determine the direction of subsequent research. Most scientific activity – in Kuhn's terminology, 'normal science' – proceeds within these constraints, contrary to the earlier view, which effectively assumed that scientific development is constraint-free. The earlier view had in fact already been increasingly rejected by historians of science before Kuhn, but not, in the main, by philosophers, and *The Structure of Scientific Revolutions* forced the questions into a wider realm, lifting them out of the narrow ambit of specialist histories of science. Also recognized by some historians of science before Kuhn, but again foregrounded in thinking about science by him, was the question of the shift from one conceptual scheme to another. On Kuhn's account, this shift was not only discontinuous – in that there was no path, as it were, from the earlier paradigm to the later one – but also incommensurable. That is to say, there is no translation between the two paradigms.

Kuhn uses the analogy of a Gestalt switch to account for the shift from one paradigm to another. In Gestalt psychology, visual recognition is construed as a function of the form-generating capacity of the brain, which constructs figures and forms out of what would otherwise be discrete lines. Occasionally, there are alternative interpretations of perceptual experiences when the brain moves back and forth between the alternatives, but it is in the nature of the Gestalt that the different interpretations cannot be experienced at the same time. An example is the 'duck–rabbit' image, which can be seen either as a duck or as a rabbit, but not both at the same time:

Kuhn argues that the 'Copernican revolution' – the shift from a geocentric (Earth-centred) to a heliocentric (Sun-centred) account of the cosmos – embodies an analogous shift. It is not simply a matter of one theory replacing another, but of suddenly seeing the whole cosmos differently. Our picture of the world and our place in it changes. Kuhn's account has sometimes been read in such a way that the move from one paradigm to another is akin to a religious conversion rather than something that can be defended rationally and in terms of evidence. Kuhn himself used this analogy, but arguably as a way of capturing the experience of moving from one paradigm to another, not as something that was designed to throw light on how changes to the content of science are made. There may indeed be paradigm shifts that reflect no objectivity and are like religious conversions, but the ones that Kuhn described, which are very much the success stories of the physical sciences, are clearly not of this type. The move from Aristotelian to Newtonian to Einsteinian cosmologies is a progression with a clear rationale in terms of objectivity, which a move in the opposite direction, for example, would not be.

Still, a problem with incommensurability remains, and it is the most contentious claim in the Kuhnian account. It is also the one that harbours the deepest consequences for objectivity. The

51

general problem is that once one allows that interpretations are theoretically motivated or theoretically guided, one must allow differences in these interpretations, and this may result in differences in what counts as evidence, in what counts as demonstration, and in what counts as a satisfactory explanation. The adequacy of theories is a matter to be assessed in terms of procedures dictated by the paradigm. When paradigms change, so do these procedures. As a result, it would seem that there is no absolute set of standards by reference to which all competing theories can be compared. Kuhn has to allow that, at some level, paradigm replacement is a matter of *competing* conceptual structures, for this is what motivates the replacement. But what sense are we to make of the idea of competing conceptual structures? For if we cannot make sense of it, all we have are worldviews replacing one another for whatever reason.

Kuhn tries to keep these questions within the confines of internal assessment, arguing that, as a paradigm develops past a certain stage, it may give rise to anomalies: it increasingly fails to reconcile the phenomena with the basic theoretical and experimental precepts of the theory. When these anomalies reach a certain stage, the paradigm is said to enter a period of crisis. What is distinctive about the crisis period is that scientists begin to look outside the paradigm for alternatives, typically questioning fundamental assumptions of the existing paradigm, and in time generating a rival paradigm.

There are three things to note as far as questions of objectivity are concerned. First, on Kuhn's account, the replacement of one paradigm by another is not a perpetual process. It is possible for a paradigm to get it right, so to speak, to resolve all the questions that it set out to solve. In such a case, the paradigm is a success, and it remains as a complete and permanent feature of scientific understanding. Kuhn gives the example of geometrical optics in the 19th century as a successful paradigm whereby all the basic problems to which the paradigm was devoted were solved and the development of the paradigm came to an end.

Second, the traditional view had secured objectivity by effectively assuming that the only issues in comparing scientific theories were empirical adequacy and explanatory power (often equated with predictive power). But what the cases of scientific revolutions highlight is that a major and radical scientific development can result from deciding that the wrong questions have been asked up to that point, and asking different questions. Objectivity is clearly beside the point if one is not asking the right questions. It is true that there are some accounts of scientific method on which the correct methodological procedures are self-correcting: that is, while in itself a procedure such as induction – inferring a general thesis from observation of individual cases – is not guaranteed to generate the correct results, repeated application of the procedure will eventually weed out errors. But there is no way in which repeated application of such a procedure is going to yield the right *questions*, because the procedure is locked in to particular questions. Any satisfactory account of objectivity must take account of the complex factors that surface in the sciences at various stages of their development: questions about what counts as an explanation, for example, and what counts as evidence. Such variations do not in themselves necessarily undermine objectivity.

Third, accounts of scientific development that, in the wake of *The Structure of Scientific Revolutions*, focus on conceptual schemes, have explored just what objectivity amounts to in the case of internal criteria for deciding on the merits of a scientific research programme. The philosopher of science Imre Lakatos, for example, set out to refine internalist criteria for assessment by specifying more precisely and in some detail the difference between progressive research programmes and degenerating research programmes. His aim was to deal with questions of assessment without having to appeal to criteria that spanned quite different kinds of project. One such criterion that Lakatos and

Kuhn rejected was that which Popper had argued for, namely falsification. Popper had treated falsification as absolute: if one proposed a theory and found evidence that contradicted it, then the theory had to be abandoned. But once cases of successful theory development in the history of science were subjected to detailed scrutiny, it quickly became evident that this was not always a promising path to follow. We have already looked at one such case, that of Galileo on the arguments for heliocentrism. While science was thought of as being simply a question of comparing competing theories with unproblematic evidence, it wore its objectivity on its sleeve, so to speak, and, as an account of the world, it was a paragon of reliability. The kinds of complexities generated by conceptual schemes considerations certainly undermine this simple picture, for what counts as appropriate evidence, for example, may be something that cannot be decided except by the theory in question. The tides were considered irrelevant to the question of whether the Earth moves before the 17th century, for instance, whereas they were a crucial piece of evidence for Galileo, Descartes, and Newton. These extra complexities do not militate against objectivity. Rather, they serve to alert us to the fact that objectivity can be contextually dependent in various ways.

Chapter 6
Is it possible to represent things objectively?

We have seen that two components in knowledge can be distinguished, justification and truth. Objectivity comes under justification, not under truth. It turns out that justification is not as straightforward as it might first appear, however. In particular, the idea that objectivity is simply a question of comparing a belief or theory with the evidence, and rejecting it if it conflicts with that evidence, does not turn out to be workable in many cases, and these include the cases where a great deal is at stake, ones in which the respective merits of significantly different theories are being assessed. Objectivity has to be adjusted accordingly, to take account of this added complexity.

But perhaps there is another way of thinking about objectivity, one that avoids these complications by bypassing questions of justification, and focuses instead on what might be taken as the positive aim of objectivity, namely an accurate representation of the world. This is how many philosophers have seen the question, at least in recent decades. If we take this path, the proposal is that we distinguish between objective and non-objective theories in terms of those theories that represent reality as it is and those that fail to do this. If we could think of objectivity not in negative terms, as with freedom from bias or prejudice, but in positive terms of the faithfulness of theories to how things are, we would have an external check on our theories, instead of an internal one.

We must ask ourselves here, however, whether in trying to do this what we are really talking about is truth rather than objectivity. These are not the same thing. One can arrive at true theories in a non-objective way. Indeed, one could hit upon the truth purely at random. Conversely, objective theories are not necessarily true. The history of science provides plenty of examples of the objective formulation and defence of theories that have turned out to be false and have been replaced by other theories. Objectivity is no guarantee of truth, any more than truth can only be the outcome of objectivity. A theory that represents things as they are is thereby true, but it is not thereby objective.

Nor can we simply say that objective theories are theories that aim at truth. Every theory aims at truth, in the trivial sense that someone who proposes a theory proposes it as a true theory, yet some theories rely on objective procedures in their formulation and some do not. Objectivity provides a particular way of pursuing enquiry, one that requires a degree of indifference in judging that may conflict with our needs and desires. How did such an approach come to take on the prominence it has, and what is its relation to truth?

Objectivity as an alternative to truth

Objectivity came to the fore in the late 16th and early 17th centuries. This is not to say that it had not been both valued and debated prior to that. But it was then that it took on a central role. The modern understanding of objectivity arose in the 16th and 17th centuries, and it arose in the context of a new concern with justification. Justification has traditionally played a central role in accounts of knowledge. Since Plato's time, knowledge has been defined as justified true belief. If we can be said to know something, we must believe it, since we cannot be said to know something if we do not believe it. Moreover, the belief must be true, since we cannot be said to know something that is false.

The interplay between justification and truth is complex, however. If the truth of a belief has been established in advance, and our task is to provide the requisite justification for it, then we have some goal for our justification, so to speak. So, for example, in the 16th and 17th centuries, Christian theologians believed that there were truths, established by a combination of biblical exegesis, common sense, and traditional teaching, about the place of the Earth in the cosmos: the Earth was stationary at the centre. Observational results or scientific theories that suggested otherwise had, the Church claimed, simply failed in their task of reconciling their results with established truth. In the first half of the 17th century, however, this strategy of reconciliation failed dramatically. The truth of the traditional doctrine could no longer be taken as being given in advance, and there was a move away from knowledge as a form of consolidation in favour of more open-ended forms of observational and experimental forms of enquiry.

If a truth is not given independently, as something with which to compare our scientific conclusions, this puts justification in a very different light, for the procedures of justification with which our theory works now need an internal vindication. But here we encounter a deep philosophical problem. On the one hand, justification, if it is to count as genuine justification in the first place, must, it seems, be driven by truth in some sense. To capture what justification is, and what we want it to do, we have to constrain what counts as a justification. It looks as if, unless we find some way of giving truth an independent role to play, in which it steers or guides justification, then we will not be able to distinguish between genuine justification and spurious, merely verbal, justification. After all, there are many ways in which we might attempt to justify a theory: we might point to the weight of tradition behind it, to its novelty, to its close fit with other things we believe, to its usefulness, and so on. The risk we run if we leave justification free of truth is that what counts as a justification will vary radically, and may include criteria that are not even cognitive in the requisite sense; they may require faith, the stamp of an arbitrarily instituted authority, and so on.

If truth does not guide the justification we offer for a theory, how do we avoid cognitively irrelevant or inappropriate justifications? The problem is that, where we have no pre-given truth with which we must reconcile our justification, then justification is all we have to go on, so that, other things being equal, what we aim for is the theory that has the greatest degree of justification. This aim has content, and it is open to assessment whether it is merely an idle claim in particular cases, for example, by contrast with the idea that we aim at true theories, which is not. Indeed, some philosophers have argued, on the basis of considerations like these, that truth just is justified belief. There is a case to be made that these are not in fact the same thing, but this is not to say that we are to understand justification in terms of how it secures truth: justification has a stand-alone quality, and cannot be analysed in terms of truth. In a scientific context, for example, if we ask whether some theory is true, what we need to be given is the justification offered for holding that theory. We can do no more in establishing its truth than establish what its justification is, where this justification is judged against what are taken to be the standards of justification for a theory of that kind making that kind of claim. Truth does not play a role here: justification is doing all the work, and now seems to provide our only guide to what theories we should prefer.

In short, truth cannot offer cognitive guidance for justification, because we cannot find out what the truth is independently of the justification. In general terms, what we want from cognitive guidance is something that makes sure that cognitively irrelevant or inappropriate considerations do not determine the direction of a justification. If truth cannot provide general cognitive guidance in science, we must look for something different from truth. The problem with truth *per se* is that the only way in which it can provide cognitive guidance is by offering some goal at which argument must aim, but the goal is not given prior to the argument. What we need instead is something that guides arguments by making sure they start and proceed in the right way, as opposed to finishing in the right way.

What happened was that, in the 17th century, objectivity replaced truth in the role of cognitive guidance. If truth guided argument by showing where arguments should end, objectivity took the opposite route, constraining how arguments should begin and proceed. It was in the newly devised notion of objectivity, in which legal argument played the most important single role, that cognitive guidance was now sought. Objectivity was deemed to be able to play this role through the qualities of impartiality, freedom from prejudices, lack of bias, and lack of partisanship.

On this way of thinking, objectivity is something quite separate from truth. Yet we still might worry that the two cannot be *wholly* unconnected, and philosophers and others have tried to establish some connection between objectivity and truth. Indeed, from the 18th century onwards, we find a move away from a negative understanding of objectivity as freedom from prejudice or bias, towards the positive idea that objectivity consists in accurate representation. While the negative conception distances objectivity from truth, the positive one brings them together in an apparent area of overlap, for accurate representation can be thought of both in terms of truth and in terms of objectivity.

Accurate representation

In their book *Objectivity*, Lorraine Daston and Peter Galison have looked in depth at how conceptions of scientific objectivity, conceived as accurate representation, have developed over the last two centuries. Their focus is on scientific atlases. These include floras (books describing plants, with aids for their identification such as botanical keys and line drawings that illustrate the distinguishing characters of the different plants), books of anatomical drawings, star maps, moon atlases, and various representations of physical processes such as interactions captured in cloud chambers. What is instructive about the study is that Daston and Galison are concerned with notions of objectivity that have come closest to embodying the actual assumptions behind procedures used in scientific investigation. They investigate a number of practical considerations that affect how one secures objectivity, considerations that are absent from more philosophical discussions, yet which turn out to be crucial in understanding what objectivity is. Above all, they indicate that, where accurate representation is concerned, securing objectivity is just one of a number of considerations which have to be traded off against one another. As they point out, objectivity is costly: in different contexts, securing objectivity in scientific atlases may demand sacrifices in pedagogical efficacy, colour, depth of field, and even diagnostic utility.

We can trace the development of four leading views on what the objectivity of a representation consists in. Although there is some overlap, there is a chronological sequence. The first development is the idea of objectivity as capturing and revealing something hidden in nature, removing all the purely accidental or contingent features of things so as to represent their essential nature, something obscured if we confine our attention to particular samples. Consider anatomical atlases. The skeletons depicted show no defects of the bones, or any of the signs of ageing that would be evident in an actual skeleton, for example. Similarly with the illustrated flora, where plant species are represented in terms of illustrations of what are in effect ideal types. The poet, dramatist, and naturalist Goethe was one of the staunchest proponents of this first conception, seeking to uncover archetypes of which all extant specimens were developments. In the case of anatomy, he sought a 'general picture containing the forms of all animals as potential', noting that 'no particular animal can be used as our point of comparison; the particular can never serve as a pattern for the whole'. Similarly in his account of the metamorphosis of plants, published in 1790, he argues that, to depict the pure phenomenon, 'the human mind must fix the empirically variable, exclude the accidental, eliminate the impure, unravel the tangled, discover the unknown'. The illustrated flora does not depict worm-eaten leaves, malformations, obscured or under-developed features. The aim is to portray the underlying form of the plant species, not a particular specimen. The point of the illustrations is to enable one to recognize the members of the species described, but of course one cannot depict a species, only specimens. So what ends up being represented is an idealized specimen. The interesting point here is that what makes the idealized specimen more objective than any particular specimen one might choose is not a question of resemblance, on this conception, but one of capturing the essence of the plant. The 'accurate' in accurate representation is not verisimilitude, but accuracy in capturing the essentials.

These means of representation may well be more useful than any other kind; and they may have greater pedagogical value than others, for example. But the problem is whether, in representing a plant in terms of an idealized specimen, it is appropriate to talk of this as an *accurate* or an *objective* representation. Daston and Galison illustrate the question very nicely with the case of the British physicist Arthur Worthington, who from the mid-1870s to the 1890s carried out a number of experiments on the shape of droplets as they fell and hit a flat surface. His first illustrations were drawn from the image left on his retina by viewing the fall of the droplet by means of rapid light flashes. The splash showed a full and beautiful symmetry. But it showed this only because irregular and asymmetrical splashes, while recorded, were rejected for purposes of illustration as unrepresentative of the phenomenon. When Worthington started using photographic images in the 1890s, he had a sudden change of heart, for these displayed none of the symmetry that he had been so concerned to capture previously. In response, he adopted a second notion of objectivity, 'mechanical' objectivity, whereby human faculties, which had effectively idealized the phenomenon, are bypassed in favour of something that is unmediated.

Here, we have a shift from the idea that objectivity requires us to go beyond mere appearances and capture the underlying reality, to the idea that what we have to capture are precisely the appearances, because anything other than 'mere' appearances goes beyond what we can objectively determine. In fact, the matter is not always quite as clear cut as it seems, since it may in some cases be possible to use one to generate the other. Francis Galton, for example, tried to discover archetypal forms of physiognomy by taking large numbers of photographs of heads and superimposing them on one another to form a composite image, which he took to capture the essentials of a particular racial or social type. The problem is that there is both an element of arbitrariness in this, and an element of deliberate choice – one chooses which pictures to superimpose on which others, for example – and this could be construed as bias.

A more pressing question is how 'objective' mechanical objectivity can be, in its own terms. The answer is that it fails to satisfy its own criteria. Not only do lighting, focus, and a host of other factors determine the image, but as early as the 19th century, especially in the production of micrographs, it became clear that two identical photographic plates, exposed in identical light conditions, can be developed to produce radically different images. This is evident in the case of anatomical photographs, for example, where fine structures such as membranes will emerge in one image which are absent in the other. Moreover, the more sensitive one's techniques, the more readily one picks up dust particles, plate defects, and so on. Light conditions can be problematic as well where these cannot be controlled, such as in moon atlases. The formative figure in the development of microphotography, Richard Neuhauss, concluded at the end of his long career that 'a photograph can only lay claim to objectivity if it is produced by an honest, gifted micro-photographer, working according to the rules of the art, and richly endowed with patience and skill'.

There was one further move that could be made within the context of a minimalist notion of objectivity. If mechanical objectivity could not realize its own ideals of accurate pictorial representation, perhaps the problem was with the very idea of something pictorial in the first place. This is the move some of the logical positivists took, and it leads in the direction of what Daston and Galison call 'structural objectivity'. What the logical positivists sought was a view from nowhere. They considered any genuinely true scientific theory to have an objective core that can be revealed by stripping away the perspectival elements which we naturally use to frame it. This was not a completely new approach, and there had been treatments of mechanics that dispensed with visual representations (in this case, geometrical diagrams) altogether, on the grounds that geometry depends on sensory faculties to grasp connections, whereas genuine demonstrations should depend on nothing that relied on contingent features of our anatomy, physiology, or psychology. Indeed, the first textbook of modern mechanics, Lagrange's *Analytical Mechanics* (1788), boasted that it contained no pictorial representations (in this case, geometrical diagrams). But there is an issue here whether Lagrange's algebraic framing is actually a more universal presentation of the theory, or just an alternative formulation to a geometrical one. That is to say, it is unclear why abstractness should be associated with greater generality when it comes to questions of accurate representation.

A more pressing difficulty is the fact that most scientific disciplines cannot get by without visual representations, whether it be star maps, anatomical atlases, micrographs, or floras. To say that objectivity is only possible without these is to misunderstand objectivity, to conceive it as something stripped bare of judgements. Once one allows that objectivity can only be a matter of judgement, the question becomes that of how it is possible to secure objectivity in judgement.

Daston and Galison argue that the upshot of the debates over accurate representation has been a move to what they term 'trained judgement'. In contemporary science, the representation, typically one that results from very complex processes such as electron micrographs or magnetic field imaging, becomes objective through a form of doctoring or editing in which images produced in an artefactual way are removed. What, it might be asked, could be objective about such forms of doctoring or editing: surely this is the opposite of objectivity? The answer depends on what the doctoring is designed to achieve. The question of objectivity in the modern era turns – to a far greater extent than it did in the period from the 16th to the 18th centuries – on the identification and elimination of arbitrary judgements. What Daston and Galison's study shows is that, once one leaves the realm of speculative epistemology, objectivity is an extremely difficult question, and in practice it is often a question of balancing various conflicting considerations rather than finding a single absolute standard.

Degrees of objectivity

The idea that objectivity in modern science consists in the elimination of arbitrary judgements is a useful move beyond that of objectivity simply consisting in the elimination of prejudice or bias. This is not because we should not worry about removing prejudice and bias, but rather because a little fine-tuning is required in moving from a general conception of objectivity to one that fits the concerns of scientific practice. The problem facing properly trained scientists is not usually a general one of bias or prejudice, but something specific to the kinds of investigations they carry out. Moreover, if the identification and elimination of arbitrary judgements are of prime concern, this is important because one can devise procedures to help in this regard. By contrast, while there might be some form of general guidance on how one can avoid bias in one's judgements, this is going to be of little use, for example, in the case of producing reliable micrographs, whereas a combination of specialized training, experience, and a good knowledge of microphysics will be invaluable. Indeed, this is part of the ethos of the modern scientist. As Daston and Galison point out, towards the end of the 19th century, seminar teaching – first introduced by philologists in German universities earlier in the century – was adapted by English scientists to their own teaching needs. Students had traditionally listened passively to lectures, which were treated as authoritative in their own right. But now students were actively induced into the craft and standards of their specialties – in the laboratory, the botanical garden, the observatory, the field, and the seminar room. Specific standards of objectivity were inculcated in the training of the student through practical experience.

In other words, not only are there degrees of objectivity, but objectivity is something that can be learned and improved upon through practice. Laboratory training is just such a means of improvement in the experimental disciplines. Refinement in the application of statistical techniques to raw data is another way in which objectivity may be increased. Another example is ordinary clinical practice, which has very specific rules governing the objectivity of the procedures used, and in giving second opinions, for example, physicians explicitly start afresh each time. This is not because the original diagnosis may have brought an element of bias or prejudice to the diagnosis, but because the first physician may have missed something. Reliability of diagnosis is difficult to achieve, and going through different procedures helps establish the required reliability.

If we neglect this practical aspect of the question, we will miss a defining feature of objectivity in the modern era. In particular, the problem with thinking of objectivity exclusively in general terms, as elimination of prejudice or bias, is that it encourages an absolutist view of objectivity. The prime example of such an absolutist conception is the view from nowhere. One thing that could motivate the view from nowhere is the idea that objectivity and truth are closely connected in such a way that we should think of objectivity as getting us closer and closer to the truth, and in the limiting case reaching the truth. We might naturally think of this in terms of an increase in accuracy of representation being correlated with an increase in proximity to the truth.

There are two problems with this conception. First, the idea that we are being guided towards *the* truth is wholly misleading. What we are being guided towards are the best answers to the questions that we pose. The quality of the answers will depend on the quality of the questions, what they assume as given, what they take to be the appropriate evidence, and what they take to be the relevant form of explanation (a question we will turn to in Chapter 8). If there is one lesson to be learned from the history of science, it is that objectivity does not discriminate between good and bad questions. If you deploy objective procedures in answering a misconceived, confused, or misleading question, it is highly likely that the answer will not get you anywhere.

Second, any attempt to assimilate objectivity and truth faces the difficulty that they behave in different ways. Note in particular that objectivity comes in degrees. One theory can be more objective than another. But a theory cannot be truer than another, because truth is an absolute notion: something is either true or it is not. There can, of course, be degrees of approximation to the truth, but these are not degrees of truth, and so are wholly unlike degrees of objectivity.

So that we are not misled into simply associating objectivity and truth, it is worth highlighting one very important difference between them. Whereas truth is absolute and does not come in degrees, objectivity *only* comes in degrees. The idea of absolute objectivity is a misconception, encouraged by thinking of it as a view from nowhere. If there is no view from nowhere, there is no limiting case where, having progressively become more and more objective, a theory can finally attain absolute objectivity. Objectivity does not become like truth in the limiting case. Indeed, some of the deepest and most persistent problems for understanding objectivity arise when one tries to make it absolute, or at least inadvertently thinks of it in absolutist terms.

What we are seeking to do in imposing standards of objectivity in our judgements in modern science is to identify and separate the informative and the uninformative, with a view to producing reliable results. Objectivity is more mundane than 'the search for truth', and it is in its very mundaneness, by contrast with the 'search for truth', that its value lies.

Chapter 7
Objectivity in numbers?

Not everything that can be counted counts, and not everything that counts can be counted.

Einstein

There is a sense of 'objectivity', dominant among the logical positivists, for example, in which, as Daston and Galison put it, it designates:

the aspects of scientific knowledge that survive translation, transmission, theory change, and differences among thinking beings due to physiology, psychology, history, culture, language, and...species. Their worries about mutual intellectual comprehension were fed by mid-nineteenth century research in history, anthropology, philology, psychology, and, above all sensory physiology, which underscored how very differently humans reasoned, described, believed, and even feared.

The logical positivists believed that if our scientific theories were to be truly objective, they had to transcend not just differences of culture and language, but also those of psychology and physiology. Even though our scientific theories have been formulated by creatures who have distinctive intellectual, psychological, physiological, and cultural characteristics which shape and inform how they arrive at their theories and how they express them, the logical positivists believed that the content of the theory must be independent of these. One way to achieve this is to translate all scientific theories into a mathematical form – not a geometrical form, for this relies too much on our physiology and psychology – but a numerical or algebraic one.

The association of objectivity and quantitative methods has a long history, and since the 19th century, such methods have become extremely flexible, making them of use not just to scientists and scholars, but to managers and bureaucrats. Quantification – the translation of statements or results into a numerical or other quantitative form, for example as graphs and tables – has become so prevalent that it has been taken by many to be what it means to be scientific and objective. At the least, it is generally taken to deliver an increase in objectivity and, as a result, disciplines that aspire to be scientific, or decision-making procedures that aspire to be rigorous and objective, almost invariably take quantification as the primary route to these goals, often in the hope that this will guarantee objectivity.

There are two things at issue here. The first is the move from specialist disinterested judgement to standardization. In large part, this came with the move to global interaction and trade, where the kind of honesty and trust that had accompanied face-to-face transactions was no longer available. Where one did not know those with whom one was trading, a set of impersonal rules guiding the transactions, in accountancy practice for example, was a good substitute. These needed a common language beyond that of individual laws and customs, and arithmetic and statistics were a language that everyone engaged in these interactions could understand. They provided a universal means of communication, and they obviated the need for personal trust and judgement. What they offered was a form of objectivity that was suited to the requirements of impersonal forms of interaction. A great deal of informed judgement typically went into formulating the requisite rules and compiling the relevant statistics, so it is not as if the numerical procedures themselves exhausted questions of objectivity. But once the numerical measures were in place, it was to them, and the rules governing them, that decisions about whether proper procedure had been followed were referred. What is at issue here is universality: the idea is that everyone follows the same procedure, whatever it is.

Consider population statistics. There are questions, in taking a national census, about whether and how one includes long-term visitors, citizens resident overseas, military forces overseas, and so on. There are also groups of urban homeless people, for example, who usually cannot be counted in a census, but whose numbers one can estimate. Should one automatically add this amount to the precise figure yielded by the census, or, because it is an estimate, should one exclude it? For many purposes, it doesn't matter which procedure one uses so long as everyone uses the same procedure, especially if the point of the exercise is purely comparative, and not the allocation of services, for example. In other words, the population figures one comes up with may be objective in the sense of providing something by which population sizes can be compared, but not objective in the sense of providing a precise figure for how many people there are in a country. Each is a perfectly reasonable sense of the word 'objectivity'. The problems arise when the considerations that motivate objectivity in the sense of something that can be universally agreed to are taken to represent objectivity as such.

Here, we come to the second issue, for there is something else that might motivate the idea that quantification is the route to objectivity, namely 'neutrality'. This is also tied in with the ideal of universality, and it is very similar to the idea, which we looked at in the last chapter under the rubric of 'mechanical objectivity', that photographs are more objective than drawings. It is just that the 'mechanical' in the present case is procedural rather than physical, but otherwise the aims are the same: to secure objectivity by removing any element of judgement. This, however, is not only a misunderstanding of what quantification can do, it gives rise to a fundamental misunderstanding of what objectivity consists in.

There is no doubt that it was the introduction of mathematical methods into physics in the 17th century that played the key role in transforming it into the powerful discipline that it had become by the end of the century. The basic statements of physics, for example, have generally taken the form of equations from Galileo onwards. Among other benefits, a mathematical form allows premises to be clearly specified; it helps guard against hidden assumptions, and it provides checks against errors in reasoning. Yet only a very small fraction of the numerical expressions, tables, and formulae that abound in the 21st century are descriptions of the natural world. The vast majority simply convey results in a standardized form which allows them to be understood by a wide audience. In his *Trust in Numbers*, the historian of statistics Theodore M. Porter has argued that since the rules for collecting and manipulating numbers are widely shared, numerical information is highly transportable. Reliance on numbers and quantitative manipulation, he argues,

> minimizes the need for intimate knowledge and personal trust. Quantification is well suited for communication that goes beyond the boundaries of locality and community. A highly disciplined discourse helps to produce knowledge independent of the particular people who make it.

In other words, what is at issue is the elimination of the need to make judgements, something motivated not just by the problems that arise where there are competing judgements, but also by the very idea that a judgement might be part of an objective assessment. On this reading, quantification is a weapon in the battle to strip information of any subjective feature, where judgement is construed as inevitably subjective. We have already seen that the idea of objectivity as something which is judgement-free is mistaken. We have also noted the role of transportability of results in the context of the attempts of the logical positivists to avoid any form of representation in the communication of results. What is at stake here is much the same: translation into a quantitative form is supposed to secure transportability. But we can allow this without allowing that it also, or thereby, secures objectivity. In fact, what has tended to happen historically is that the rise in the authority of statistical and behavioural norms, applied to everything from crime and homosexuality to suicide and birth and death rates, has created a language of normality and abnormality.

In his *Trust in Numbers*, Porter explains how effective quantification has never been a matter simply of discovery, but always also of administration, hence of social and technological power. Quantitative objectivity is a form of standardization, the use of rules to confine and tame the personal and subjective. In other words, through quantification, a new realm has been created in which, rather than securing objectivity, objectivity has been created. The information has been marshalled in such a form that one can now raise questions of objectivity in a way that one could not have done before. Quantification has become a powerful tool for understanding a world that it has itself constructed.

Objectivity as a form of micro-management

A good example of this development is the use of claims to quantitative objectivity as a tool of government micro-management. In his *Thatcher and Sons* (2006), the political commentator Simon Jenkins looked at how, in the space of a couple of decades, Britain became the most regulated country in the non-communist world, with every aspect of public policy relentlessly audited.

In 1983, a government-sponsored report on the British National Health Service concluded that it was under-managed. New chief executives were appointed to take charge of the local health authorities, and they were instructed not just to succeed but to succeed measurably: they were told to log waiting lists, appointments, referrals, lengths of stay, operations, incidents, perinatal deaths, overall mortality rates, in fact anything to which a number could be attached. A new era of statistics was initiated thereby, because the central tenet of these new developments was that only the measurable is manageable, and the aim was to manage. By the 1990s, this micro-managerial strategy was being applied to the police through legislation introduced to authorize the Home Office to set targets for the police and to publish the success rates of the various forces in meeting these targets. Anything that could be measured was measured, and recorded crime was picked out as a particularly important statistic, even though recording it manifestly varied as a function of such factors as police station opening hours and readiness among members of the public to pick up a phone. Changes such as the creation of new offences, new definitions of vandalism, minor changes in insurance rules, and the opening of new call centres or closing of old ones, all had a very significant impact on the statistics. Yet the targets set were numerically precise. This was true not just of the targets set for the police, but now for virtually every public utility. The Atomic Energy Commission was told to increase the proportion of favourable media coverage by 43.9%, while the Foreign Office had a numerical target set for 'global peace and stability'.

With the compilations of statistics and the introduction of targets, audits and league tables inevitably emerged. Sometimes the audits completely missed the point. In 2005, the prime minister announced that 99.89% of patients had been able to get an appointment with their GP within 48 hours as a result of new procedures, which included bonuses for GPs who saw their patients within this time. This spectacular 'success' was achieved by GPs never making an appointment for more than 48 hours ahead. Patients who were unable to get an appointment within the next 48 hours were instructed to ring back at the end of that period. Here, quantified targets do not regulate general practice, and certainly don't improve it, so much as create a new form of general practice that conforms in an artificial way to what are in effect arbitrary statistical norms.

League tables are a natural consequence of these kinds of audits. They were first adopted for school examination results, and quickly spread to university research, hospital waiting lists, infant mortality, heart disease, and police performance. The rapid emergence of league tables reveals something at the heart of the audit/target culture, namely the way in which reliance on raw statistical information, collected without due consideration of the subject matter, acts to standardize, and indeed homogenize, information. No wonder that management techniques introduced in the National Health Service could be applied so readily to the police, that league tables for school results could be applied so readily to planning approvals and fertility clinic success. It is not that there is a natural affinity between these areas. What has happened instead is that they have been divested of their content, which has been replaced by a new micro-manageable one, which in many cases bears little relation to the original aims of the public utilities.

The reduction of things to raw numbers has affinities with the view that the most objective observations are those which have been stripped of all judgements and laid bare. The consequences of this misconception are most evident in the cases we have just looked at. It is not so much that quantification – in this case, the reduction of things to numbers, to statistical regularities, so that everything can be put on the same level and compared – becomes tantamount to objectivity. It is not even so much that such objectivity now becomes a tool for micro-management. Rather, it becomes a form of control that allows complete abdication of responsibility. The numbers speak for themselves!

Politicians and bureaucrats are no longer responsible for the decisions made, because all elements of personal judgement have been removed.

Quantification as an aid to judgement

It is evident that there are significant dangers in allowing quantification to replace judgement, allowing it to usurp the title of objectivity from a properly considered disinterested opinion given by someone with the relevant experience and skills. This does not mean that quantification has no part to play in decision-making in the social and political realms, however. The difference is that, in the cases we just considered, quantitative methods replace sound judgements. But there are genuine cases where such methods complement judgements, and can actually help us in reaching sound judgements.

These cases are those of allocation of resources in conditions of uncertainty. Perhaps the best-known example is triage. When one attends an accident and emergency department of a hospital, the severity of one's injuries are assessed by a triage nurse. Triage is a process that was devised by French doctors in World War I (although it had precedents going back to Napoleon) for determining the priority of patients' treatments depending on the severity of their condition. There are basically three categories of patient: those who are likely to live even if they receive no treatment; those who are likely to die unless they receive treatment; and those who are likely to die whether they receive treatment or not. With sufficient resources, everything turns on the severity of the case, and patients in all three categories can be treated. But once we consider a situation with scarce resources, the ordering of priorities can no longer be based simply on the urgency of the case. Now we need to trade off an assessment of the urgency of the case against the probability of success. In a situation of especially scarce resources, such as on a battlefield, patients in the third category may well be left to die. It is, of course, possible to reject triage as fundamentally immoral, on the grounds that leaving someone to die, when there is the slightest possibility that he or she can be saved, is unacceptable. However, if, as a result of attention to a small number of injured whose chances of survival are low, we endanger a larger number who would have had a high probability of surviving had we directed all our attention to them, this is an outcome most would consider outweighs any claim to start with the most seriously injured, irrespective of the probability of success. Probability of success is the key point. Given we can estimate probability of success and degree of injury, the problem now arises how we combine these in such a way that we are able to make a reliable decision.

Here, the answer is to be found in a quantitative discipline, decision theory, which provides us with a means of combining these two. In the language of decision theory, at issue here are 'expected utilities': for example, the value we place on saving someone who will die if we do not act, compared with the value we place on someone who might survive if we do not act. Decision theory is a quantitative method that looks abstruse and alien in matters of vital ethical importance. But actually, so long as we take it as an aid to decision-making, and not a substitute for decision-making, it is of inestimable help. Decision theory is a theory about making decisions under conditions of uncertainty. In particular, it offers a simple way of calculating the 'utility' of any particular action, and it has a crucial feature: instead of just dealing with raw utilities, the formula incorporates a figure for the probability of success, combining the two in a precise way so that the guidance is now fine-tuned to the problem of allocation of resources. It is no longer simply a question of working on the principle that it is better to save someone who will certainly die without intervention, irrespective of the chances of success, rather than devote scarce resources instead to less serious cases. Everything depends on what the chances of success are in saving the critically injured person. Consider the case on a World War I battlefield where these chances are small but where the chances of preventing a far larger number of less seriously injured from death are high. Then the decision rule may indicate that we need to abandon the critically injured in order to prevent many others who are presently not so threatened.

The range of cases in which decision theory may prove helpful extends far beyond medical triage, to any case where there is allocation of scarce resources. Consider the decisions that a conservation manager has to make. She has limited resources, so needs to make a decision about how to spend these resources. Let us imagine there are three grades of species conservation status: not threatened, near threatened, and threatened. The allocation decision questions clearly arise in the case of the last two. How is this to be done? One way to proceed would be to devote the resources to the most pressing problems, namely the most endangered species. These are, after all, going to be wiped out in the immediate future if one does not act now. But this might not be a sensible use of resources. Saving only the most threatened species may prove very costly, and may affect only a small number of individual animals, using up available resources. Species not previously threatened might now move into the threatened category, but not be supportable since the resources have been exhausted. Clearly, some kind of calculation is necessary. More generally, any allocation of scarce resources, such as government allocation of spending on health, education, and defence, for example, is subject to the same considerations.

There is a crucial difference between this kind of case and the 'numbers say it all' cases that we looked at earlier. In the earlier cases, quantification – above all, translation into numerical form – replaces judgements because it is believed that judgements, no matter how carefully reasoned and how much expertise and skill are relied upon, have an element of subjectivity which undermines their objectivity. By contrast, in the use of quantitative methods to help in deciding allocation of scarce resources, such methods are not substituted for sound judgements. Rather, they are employed as a help in reaching sound judgements, for example in a case where our natural intuition might lead us to believe that we should always save the most threatened first, an intuition almost certainly formed on the implicit assumption of a world of certainties, rather than one beset by uncertainty, where our untutored intuitions have little purchase.

Chapter 8
Can the study of human behaviour be objective?

Explaining human behaviour prompts us to reflect on the nature of objectivity, because it raises questions about the form objectivity takes once we go beyond the natural sciences. Consider the case of an anthropologist studying a rain dance. We can safely assume that rain dances could not actually cause it to rain, and that the lack of correlation between the dances and rainfall would be evident to any disinterested observer. Yet the dance is always performed at times of drought. What are we to make of this? Assume that there is evidence that, in times of drought, social strife and uncertainty about the nature of authority increases. Because the dance does not bring success in what the dancers consider to be its aim, we might argue that the reason for the dance should be given in functionalist terms: it secures social cohesion at a time when this is at risk. But there is also a sense in which this explanation is a wholly inappropriate: the dancers perform the rain dance only when they want it to rain, and their reason for performing it is clearly that they believe that it will increase the chance of rain. Are we sacrificing explanatory plausibility in proceeding with a functionalist explanation? Surely an account of their behaviour that neglects this is not going to be satisfactory. Suppose we are trying to explain the rain dance to someone who is completely unfamiliar with the phenomenon: could we be said to have offered something informative if it did not even mention the intention on the part of the dancers to make it rain?

We have a choice between two types of explanation here. This is not necessarily a choice in the sense that the two are mutually exclusive. They ask different questions, and generate different forms of understanding. But if these are not mutually exclusive, they do seem to involve different commitments to objectivity. Up to this point, we have considered objectivity in everyday general terms, and in terms of what objectivity amounts to in scientific practice, and the general understanding of objectivity that we have worked with requires us to stand back from the phenomena we are examining, as it were, so that we can investigate and assess them from a wholly impartial standpoint, one that could be used for any phenomena of this kind. If we were to insist on this understanding in the present case, then we could only allow the functionalist explanation, for by these criteria, only the functionalist explanation is objective and impartial. What seems to mark out functional explanation is that it is a kind of explanation that is sufficiently general for it to work in the same way in any society. By contrast, the explanatory value of a localized explanation, which takes its starting point from a set of beliefs and practices which have no universal standing, would seem minimal. How could it do more than just repeat, effectively in their own words, what the dancers believe about the point of the dance?

Yet there is something unsatisfactory about denying any objectivity to the non-functionalist anthropologist's localized account in this way. To highlight the issue, consider the case of a particularly crude functionalism, where it is simply a matter of imposing a universal grid on a broadly identified class of rituals, without any investigation of particular cases. Chemistry might be taken as a model here: if someone mixes hydrochloric acid and sodium hydroxide, we know the reaction will produce sodium chloride and water. There is nothing of an individual nature about the reagents, and we do not need to investigate the particular physical reaction to understand what is happening. So too the idea is that variations in rituals are superficial, and their core is always functional: social cohesion is paramount in any society, and rituals are one of the most effective ways of achieving this, especially in a primitive society. The lack of any interest in detail or individual variations here stands in marked contrast to the anthropologist who visits the tribe, learns their language, examines their distinctive social structure, looks at how their rituals fit with one another, and who, as a result of this, offers an empirically rich account that captures something distinctive about the tribe and their behaviour. On this account of their activities, the anthropologist is certainly taking far greater care in searching for an explanation than the functionalist is, and empirical factors play a crucial role, in a way they do not in the crude functionalist account, where it is simply a question of fitting things into a pre-arranged scheme.

The claims of functionalism to objectivity rest very centrally on the analogies between the way in which it deals with its subject matter and the way in which the natural sciences deal with their subject matter. Yet that social actors are unlike chemical reagents is clear from the fact that, as well as a functionalist account, one can offer a very different kind of explanation of their behaviour, whereas chemical explanation is all there is to offer in the case of the reaction. The dilemma we face is that there are good independent grounds for considering the anthropologists' procedures as seeking to achieve objectivity, for example in their concern with empirical detail, yet the principle of distancing oneself from one's object of study seems to be violated in such an approach to anthropology. The question this raises is whether this principle can be jettisoned, or at least mitigated, in the case of the human sciences.

Universal explanation versus local interpretation

Let us begin by considering the more general implications of accepting only functionalist explanations in the case of social behaviour. Functionalism works on the idea that we must stand back from the phenomena and treat them as we would any other of the same kind. In the light of this requirement, consider the case where the functionalist sets out to convince one of the dancers that what the rain dance is about is really social cohesion, not rain. She shows the dancer the statistics on correlations between rain and dances; she introduces him to basic anthropological theory, sets out a general account of social cohesion which is universal in its scope; and she uses a number of examples to illustrate the widely varying, but identifiable, responses to problems of social cohesion. Let us say that the dancer is finally convinced, and acknowledges that what the rain dances have been about is not rain, after all, but social cohesion.

In the course of his education, assume that the dancer has also picked up quite a bit of knowledge about Western culture and its political systems. He immediately sees parallels between the latter and his own society's rain dances. He sees that, for many decades, there has been a convergence in the policy programmes of the main political parties, that is, those with a realistic chance of gaining power, and, because of the constraints of office, an even greater convergence in the policies actually adopted once the party has been elected to government. He is struck by the fact that regular parliamentary or presidential elections elect people with similar policies every time (relative to the political spectrum). There are many other analogies between elections and rain dances. Just as different tribes paint themselves in distinctive colours which differentiate them from one another while performing the dance, so Western political parties adopt different colours for their parties. And just as it is the head man who decides when it is time to perform the rain dance, so it always seems to be the head man who calls elections in Western societies. Could it be, the dancer wonders, that regular elections are like regular rain dances, a means not of changing something – the weather or government policies – but rather a means of securing social cohesion? He realizes that regular elections could in theory change government policies significantly in a way that rain dances could not change the weather, but is struck by the fact that they rarely do so. The odds of a significant change of government policy following an election is about the same as a downpour following a rain dance. He decides the question is the same in both cases: if it doesn't make any difference (on average), why do the participants keep doing it?

On the basis of what he has been taught about looking beyond local explanations to something truly general that underlies various social practices, whatever their provenance, the dancer concludes that elections are a means of securing social cohesion, and that the beliefs and intentions of voters do not bear on the phenomenon. To his great puzzlement, or perhaps amusement, the functionalists and others who had taught him to view the customs of his own culture scientifically, at the same time pointing out the difficulties of participants in accepting this, are singularly resistant to having the same standards applied to their own culture. They insist that such a view of Western political systems is unduly cynical, and that while such a view may be held by minority groups of radicals, for example, hardly anyone regards such a functionalist account of Western politics as a plausible full explanation. But he points out in response that those groups of radicals proceed on the basis of a general social theory which, however counterintuitive it might be to most of the participants in liberal democracies, could hardly be opposed on these grounds since that is precisely what is at issue in functionalist explanations of rain dances.

Functionalist explanations can, of course, be a good deal more sophisticated than in this imaginary example, but we have enough here to appreciate that there might be something asymmetrical about the way in which they are applied. It might be argued in response that functionalism is a scientific theory, unlike more local explanations, and because of this, it embodies an objectivity that enables it to rise above cultural differences. In the same way that mathematical, physical, astronomical, and (perhaps) economic theories are able to offer a neutral and comprehensive vantage point, so anthropological theories can provide something that does not reflect Western culture but in some sense transcends it. But this is to assume that scientific explanation is always of a general nature, and that there are no local explanations that are complete in themselves. This is a questionable assumption.

There is also a deeper problem, however, which is that, in making these claims for the superiority of Western anthropology over local explanations, we need to be sure that we are not simply exporting local Western values in the guise of universal ones. The potential danger is that the very idea of an anthropology of this kind creates something in a particular image, rather than capturing something that is actually there.

A good analogy is with the classification of religions in the Christian West. Before the 17th century, Western theologians did not recognize different religions and treated Islam and Judaism, in particular, as forms of heresy, but in the course of the 17th and 18th centuries, there were attempts to distinguish other religions from Christianity. Then again in the 19th century, there was a concerted move to offer comprehensive classifications of world religions. The classifications were very much from within Christianity, and the different religions were distinguished on a doctrinal basis. This is where the question of creating something in a particular image arises.

Christianity is in fact quite unique in its construal of the identity of a religion as lying in its beliefs. For Christianity, it is necessary and sufficient to be a Christian that one have particular beliefs, and it was assumed that this criterion was shared with the other world religions. But it is not shared. In Islam, Buddhism, Confucianism, Hinduism, and Judaism, for example, particular daily rituals, practices (such as meditation and chanting), striving to attain balance and order, or a notion of return from exile, are the crucial things. These are sometimes in conjunction with certain beliefs, sometimes not: the crucial thing is that the beliefs alone are not sufficient, and are often not even necessary. Confucianism does not even posit the existence of a god, and what is distinctive of this religion for its practitioners is rather the transition from chaos to order. Even when a god is posited, belief in the existence of that god may not be a necessary condition for belonging to that religion, as in Judaism. In short, the doctrinal focus of Christianity is something peculiar to Christianity. Any attempt here to secure objectivity by trying to be neutral about which doctrines are the correct ones is misguided, because the problem lies at a deeper level, namely that of construing religions in terms of doctrines in the first place. The question a functionalist anthropology has to answer is whether it is doing the same kind of thing, assuming that social acts in different cultures must all have something in common, must all ultimately be doing the same kind of thing, even if the parties to such social acts would not recognize the descriptions offered.

I do not want to suggest that there is a simple solution to these dilemmas. Far from it. What the cases show is the need for the exercise of judgement, instead of blindly relying on a mode of explanation which had been identified as 'scientific' or 'objective' independently of context.

Explanation and interpretation

A second kind of response to the problems raised by functionalism is to abandon the claim that this is the only kind of account that can proceed objectively, and to insist that objectivity might actually require us to adopt the values of the participants. To return to the rain dance example, the argument is that the functionalist account fails to – indeed cannot but fail to – capture the thought that motivates the participants in the dance. One way in which this contrast is sometimes expressed is in terms of the distinction between reasons and causes: giving the reasons someone has for doing something (or interpreting the behaviour) and giving the causes of their behaviour are two different things.

The difference is between appropriate interpretation of the behaviour and appropriate explanation of it. The former has to answer to how the actors themselves conceive of what they are doing, whereas the latter does not.

Certain philosophers, most notably Giambattista Vico (1668–1744) and Wilhelm Dilthey (1833–1911), have argued that the natural sciences and the human sciences are quite distinct in this respect. In particular, while it might be appropriate to 'stand back' from phenomena in the natural sciences to achieve objectivity, this is inappropriate in the case of the human sciences, where we are dealing not with an objectified realm, but with human beings who have intentional states, emotions, the ability to exercise judgement, and so on. These are attributes that they share with the investigator, and which the investigator is therefore in a position to interpret and of which he or she can make sense. This is something quite different from what we do in the natural sciences. On this view, to take the functionalist road would be to treat the rain dance as if it were on a par with a natural, non-intentional phenomenon. It would thus fail to appreciate the nature of the phenomenon under investigation. In other words, what is being argued is that the physical sciences have been taken to provide a model of objectivity *per se*, something that can simply be exported to any other area of study.

The fact that there are no cases in physics that correspond to the explanatory dilemmas that arise in accounting for the rain dance, for which application of a model of explanation directly based on that of physics generates such problems, suggests that there is something inappropriate about the model here. Proponents of the view that there is a sharp distinction between the natural sciences and the human sciences are not denying that objectivity in the sense of impartiality is appropriate in the human sciences. Rather, they are denying that criteria of objectivity, or guides as to how objectivity might be achieved, can simply be imported from the natural sciences, because what is at stake is not the discovery of causes but the interpretation of behaviour.

It is far from clear that either of these approaches provides the 'right answer'. This would be to assume that there is just one way of explaining the rain dance. Rather, different accounts bring to light different aspects of the phenomenon. The success of an explanation is relative to what one wants explained, and there is no reason why the choices should be restricted to two mutually exclusive accounts. There is a deep question here about just how significantly the means by which objectivity is to be secured can vary. But the nature of objectivity itself is not in dispute. What is at issue is how objectivity in the human sciences is best achieved, not whether objectivity consists in something different in the natural and human sciences. Whether one is seeking to discover the causes of behaviour or to interpret it, what we seek is an impartial account, one which could ideally be accepted by any subject on the basis of evidence and/or arguments.

General models of understanding

An alternative to functionalist and 'distinctive human sciences' models is to insist that there is a general model applicable to all investigations that aspire to be objective, but that it is different from the natural sciences model. One way one might proceed is to argue that the model taken from the natural sciences fails to penetrate deeply enough into just what is crucial to the conception of understanding with which the natural sciences work. The problem is whether one can offer something more general that correlates with the notion of objectivity.

A recent example of a model that is seemingly derived from the natural sciences, but which is actually in many respects closer to that of the human sciences, is Barbara Herrnstein Smith's response to attempts to offer naturalistic accounts of religion. Among her targets are the work of two anthropologists, Pascal

Boyer and Scott Atran, who have offered evolutionary explanations of the persistence of religion in the modern age. Boyer, for example, has argued that the operation of human minds was shaped early in our evolution by categories of agent-detection, and by 'ontological categories', which are basic divisions of nature into animals, plants, tools, and so on. Agent-detection, he argues, evolved to alert our ancestors to the possible presence of prey or predators, and it was of necessity a hypersensitive device, which had the result that humans were led to posit animate agents of some kind even when there were none. Accompanying this agent-detection mechanism is an inference system that automatically supplies such agents with particular characteristics or properties based on the basic 'ontological categories', with the result that we generate watchful ancestors, angry gods, and so on. Atran supplements this evolutionary psychology approach with a quasi-functionalist account whereby the religious sensibility that is the outcome of these developments has a functional explanation; it meets enduring emotional and societal needs, as well as maintaining the moral codes required for social order.

Smith's response is not to follow defenders of the idea that there is a sharp contrast between explanations appropriate to the natural sciences and those appropriate to the human sciences. She argues that this is a misguided way of trying to explain religious sensibilities not because it applies a scientific model but because of the particular scientific model it applies. Her main criticism is that the scientific model that has been used in these cases is too narrow. Following the work of early 20th-century historian of science Ludwig Fleck (who has often been regarded as elaborating many of the theses that Kuhn was subsequently to take up), Smith argues that:

> what we come to call the truth or validity of some statement – historical report, scientific explanation, cosmological theory, and so forth – is best seen not as its objective correspondence to an

autonomously determinate external state of affairs but, rather, as our experience of its consonance with a system composed of already accepted ideas, already interpreted and classified observations, and, no less significantly, the embodied perceptual and behavioural dispositions that are thereby engendered and constrained.

This is the general model that Smith extracts from science, and, on this model, 'religion', construed as a way of organizing our world in terms of the sacred, effectively comes out as being as objective as the natural sciences. Even if one were happy with religion coming out this way, however, I cannot see how one might limit what is to be included in religion here. Devotion to science-fiction characters such as Jeddi knights could act as a way of organizing one's world by providing a sense of the sacred, and there is at least one religion, Scientology, that has its basis in science fiction. With a little ingenuity, even practices that, at least in common-sense terms, no one would regard as religious, such as support for sports teams (which actually have occasionally been modelled on religions by some sociologists), could be construed as being on a par with science along these lines. What is offered is simply too general to exclude anything, and fails to meet the demands of any of the notions of objectivity that we have examined. We end up with a manifest form of relativism.

Chapter 9
Can there be objectivity in ethics?

It is not too difficult to understand the role of objectivity in science and in scholarship. Morality is a different case. In the medieval West, for example, morality was centred around the seven deadly sins: wrath, greed, sloth, pride, lust, envy, and gluttony. It is not clear where objectivity would come into this story. It is not as if avoiding the vices and embracing the virtues they mirror—patience, charity, diligence, humility, chastity, kindness, temperance—is in any sense acting *objectively*. Objectivity does not seem an especially appropriate way of thinking about morality. One might argue about whether pride is really a vice, for example, but in doing so, one would not appeal to objectivity. In particular, what role could impartiality or freedom from bias play in moral reasoning? Morality, it might be argued, is about right and wrong, and these are not matters that we decide by balancing various options; and certainly not by removing any consideration of values from our moral judgements.

In fact, there are a number of ways in which objectivity and morality have come to be associated since the 17th century, and one development stands out from the rest in importance. This is the shift from a religious to a secular conception of morality at exactly the time when the objectivity of religious beliefs was being called into question. Objectivity and secularization are, historically speaking, intimately tied, and the history here is revealing.

The problem of moral diversity

One of the characteristic features of Enlightenment thought is the emerging use of empirical methods, sometimes mirroring those of the physical sciences, to open up questions that had traditionally occupied the realms of humanist learning and religious doctrine. What lay behind these developments was a concern to come to terms with cultural difference and moral diversity. From the end of the 16th century, with the appearance of travel books describing non-European lands and peoples, the possibility began to be raised—slowly at first, but coming to a head by the last decades of the 17th century—that a number of fundamental beliefs that had been taken to be universal were in fact culturally variable. Religion and morality were at the centre of this questioning.

It was generally assumed in the 17th century that religion provided the unique basis for morality, and that without religion, there could be no morality. It was also taken as given that not only had all cultures embraced religion of one kind or another, but also that no great thinker had ever espoused atheism. But there were growing doubts, and matters came to a head in the 1690s with the publication of Bayle's defence of the possibility of a virtuous atheist. Bayle denied that religion was in fact universal and that it was something that attracted unanimous agreement. More radically, he also pointed out that, even if it were, this would in itself not constitute irrefutable grounds for accepting its legitimacy. Religion, Bayle argued, is neither necessary nor sufficient for morality, and a society of atheists would still be governed by the desire for honour and reputations, as well as rewards and punishments.

At the same time, the various practices of 'primitive' peoples that John Locke culled from the travel literature—child murder, parricide, cannibalism, and incest—threw doubt on whether there was indeed any underlying moral uniformity and, combined with his very influential full-scale attack on innate ideas, the view that there was a religious morality present in everyone at birth began to look less and less plausible. Some writers, like the 18th-century French political theorist Baron de Montesquieu, concluded from travel reports that moral diversity was so widespread that morals varied depending on national, cultural, and even climatic, factors. This made morality relative, in that the truth or falsity of moral judgements was neither absolute nor universal, but relative to different traditions, convictions, religions, and so on. Prior to this time, the standard response to evidence of moral diversity had been to invoke innate ideas of what is right and wrong, but this defence was in effect no longer available in the 18th century, and it was difficult to counter relativism and to defend the view that there was at least some universality in morals.

It is in this context that we start to find considerations of objectivity entering the picture. At the beginning of the 18th century, the English theologian and philosopher Samuel Clarke tried to provide a rational foundation for Christian morality, that is, a defence of Christian morality that made no reference to Christian doctrine. He argued that what marks out Christian morality is the fact that it is the 'natural' morality: it corresponds to what is naturally right. This enabled Clarke to deal with an otherwise troubling dichotomy in ethics: he accepted that God is completely free, and orders the world in a way that is constrained by nothing, for nothing could constrain such a perfect being, while on the other hand rejecting the voluntarist view, that goodness and truth are arbitrary. Clarke urges that God's action must reflect natural standards of truth and goodness, rather than instantiate such standards arbitrarily. He attempted to reconcile these principles by means of a doctrine of the 'fitness of things', whereby nature has a moral aspect which mirrors its physical aspect, both moral and physical aspects being knowable by reason. The idea is that any rational being will guide its conduct in terms of these moral principles. Since God is completely rational, he follows these completely, but we know that we are also influenced by passions which act against reason and cause us to behave immorally on occasion, and it is from this, Clarke concludes, that the need for established religions arises.

To maintain that Christianity mirrored a natural morality could hardly settle the issue of moral diversity, however, and it raises the general question whether there could be a form of argument that enabled one rationally to decide between competing moral judgements. In the late 18th and early 19th centuries, a distinctive kind of response to this question arose, whereby one might not be able to decide between substantive moral claims, but where there was a form of moral reasoning that underlay moral judgements which was not relative. This form of moral reasoning was encapsulated in a principle of universalizability. I say a principle, because it took many forms, lying behind Kant's ethics and later the very different utilitarian ethics of the 19th century. Nevertheless, whatever the differences in the details, the general idea is clear. It is that moral judgements are universalizable: one should act towards others as one would want them to act towards oneself. In other words, it is not so much the values in their own right that are important, but the kind of justification that we can provide for them in terms of universalizability.

Note that, in this case, we would not have to claim that moral statements were true or false—had 'truth values' as philosophers put it—even though we were claiming that there were objective grounds for some of them. What is objective are the grounds on which we assert certain moral values, in that they issue from a procedure that everyone making a moral judgement should follow, and indeed, which may be implicit in the very idea of making moral judgements.

The trouble here is that the process of universalization starts from moral judgements in the first place. It is true that, as a result of asking oneself whether a particular judgement is universalizable and deciding it is not, one might decide that the judgement does not represent something moral after all, but this will not be the usual case. In the usual case, one simply has to fix on a particular starting point, yet however uncontroversial it may appear, it still may not be acceptable to others. In such cases, universalizing will not achieve genuine universality, only universality among those who accept the same premises. In other words, even if one could get everyone to agree to the principle of universalizability, this would not yield the same moral principles. At best, it would simply act to identify something as a candidate for moral judgement in the first place. What this means is that, even if one could establish a means of making moral judgements objective via the principle of universalizability, this objectivity would fail to answer the problem of moral diversity.

One might think that moral diversity, while real, affects only peripheral or localized moral values, and that there are nevertheless core moral values which are not relative, but have an absolute standing. They are objective. Not only have theologians and philosophers tried to identify these, but legislators too, most notably in modern times in the United Nations Universal Declaration of Human Rights (1948). Yet what are identified look more like prescriptions for behaviour rather than descriptions of core values that underlie actual behaviour.

A path one might take in response to this is to abandon the search for some fixed objective content to morality, and instead think of morality in terms of rules of behaviour. This was the hope of Kant and of the utilitarians, who believed that some principle of universalizability lay at the core of morality. This approach has been refined over the last half-century, especially since the publication in 1971 of John Rawls's *A Theory of Justice*. As its title indicates, this is a theory of justice, not a theory of morality, but the argument has clear implications for morality. In particular, if one is prepared to centre one's conception of morals around a social notion, such as fairness, as opposed to traditional individual virtues, then a greater degree of universality can be achieved. Rawls starts from the principle that most reasonable principles of justice are those everyone would accept and to which they would agree as fair. He asks us to imagine a situation in which societal roles are refashioned and redistributed, and that individuals, from behind the veil of ignorance, do not know what role they will be reassigned. This enables him to determine what constitutes a fair agreement in which everyone is impartially situated as equals, and in this way to determine principles of social justice. Here, we have a version of the universalizability argument which does not depend on accepting certain moral premises, but is genuinely neutral in this respect. To the extent to which it succeeds in yielding fundamental principles of fairness, it introduces a methodological universality which is both binding and, because of its universality, can make real claims to objectivity.

The problem remains, however, just what such an account tells us about morality. Acting consistently may well go to the core of a liberal notion of justice, but traditionally there has been a resistance (starting with Kant's earliest critics) to the idea that one can reduce acting morally to acting consistently. To this extent, it will not be considered to have provided an objective basis for morality. Nevertheless, it does seem that, to the extent that one seeks something objective about morality, this is the most promising route open. To reject this route may well be to relinquish any hope of connecting basic moral principles and objectivity.

There are questions here about whether any single account could secure objectivity for particular moral precepts. There seem to be notions closely associated with morality—such as universalizability, justice, and feelings of obligation and guilt— each of which can be fleshed out, if only with varying degrees of success, in objective terms. But morality itself, assuming there is some core notion of morality that goes beyond these, seems to resist such treatment. If we accept the idea that there are fundamental moral values which transcend localized moral diversity, and if we believe that the way to account for this is in terms of objectivity, then we need to ask whether we should abandon the idea that there is a core notion of morality. Perhaps we should instead treat it as being more like an interference effect of various different kinds of considerations: universalizability, justice, and feelings of obligation and guilt.

Chapter 10
Can there be objectivity in taste?

On the face of it, the issues presented by trying to establish objectivity look very much the same in aesthetics as in ethics. If we take our core understanding of what it is to be objective from the natural sciences, for example, then the respects in which both moral judgements and judgements of taste differ from this look similar. In particular, there is a widespread belief that one's own moral and aesthetic judgements are not merely relative, but that they are the products of reflection and that, as a result, they have some substance. That is, they are not *merely* products of our culture or our individual circumstances: not something that will be easily abandoned as these change, for example. On the other hand, both moral and aesthetic judgements diverge to a significantly greater extent than those we find in the natural sciences. Indeed, the degree of divergence in matters of taste seems far greater than that we find in moral judgements, and as a result, one might consider that we could deal with the issues in ethics, and then treat aesthetics as simply a more extreme case of divergence in judgements.

But in fact, there are respects in which the questions raised by aesthetic judgement are different from those that arise in the case of moral judgement. The single most important difference is that ethical judgements are not generally regarded as subjective, whereas the distinguishing feature of aesthetic judgements is precisely that they are subjective. This subjectivity is not something that simply goes beyond moral judgement, and pushes matters of taste further into the realm of relativity. Subjectivity is in some crucial respects—respects important for our understanding of aesthetic judgements—different from relativity.

Subjective values

One form of relativism is perspectivalism, the theory that everything is relative to a particular perspective from which we view or think about it. Statements about events relative to a particular time and place, for example, are perspectival but they are not necessarily subjective. If I say 'it rained here yesterday', this is manifestly relative to my place and time, since I am not claiming that this statement is true wherever and whenever it is made. But it is also objective: there is an objective fact of the matter about whether it rained at the place and time mentioned. So something can be relative and objective.

A central question in the case of taste—a question that forms the basis for the formative works of Hume and Kant on aesthetics—is the converse question: whether something can be subjective and yet not merely relative to us. This might seem a contradiction in terms. However, when we reflect on exactly what we want to capture when allowing, for example, the possibility that some judgements on matters of taste are better than others, we clearly face a dilemma if we write off taste as simply a matter of personal preference. The first thing that needs to be done is to clarify the notions of subjectivity and relativity at issue.

As a good first approximation, we can say that our aesthetic judgements are subjective in the sense that they depend on feelings of pleasure or displeasure. Were there no feelings of pleasure or displeasure that motivated our judgements, these would not be aesthetic judgements, and in this way aesthetic judgements are marked out from moral or scientific judgements, for example. The criterion would need refining if we were to delve more deeply into the matter—it seems odd to say, for example, that the aesthetic appreciation of a particularly gruelling tragedy, such as Seneca's *Medea* or Ibsen's *Ghosts*, is based on pleasure as usually understood—but for our purposes, it is sufficient to imagine how the notion might be refined once one has established the central cases. The point is that pleasure is something intrinsically subjective. Of course, one can be taught how to look at paintings, or listen to music, more thoughtfully, and one can rely on authorities to point out things one would not otherwise have picked up; as a result of this, one's pleasure on viewing or listening will be increased. When this happens, one may, having been convinced by various arguments and demonstrations, gain more pleasure as a result. But this does not lend objectivity to the pleasure. Aesthetic judgements, unlike scientific or ethical judgements, are response-relative. The judgement is triggered by a particular kind of response, namely pleasure or displeasure. This response is by its nature subjective if only because it is just that, a response: something individual and psychological.

Universal values

What, then, of the relativity of the judgement? The point about an aesthetic judgement is not that it is 'relative to me', which tells us nothing since, in some sense, every judgement I make is relative to me, but that it is disinterested. If we think of an aesthetic judgement as reflecting the pleasure found in the object, then the judgement is not motivated by inclination or desire, in the sense that desire does not produce aesthetic judgements. I cannot want to get pleasure from something and as a result actually get more pleasure from it. The pleasure itself is independent of my desires, and is not the kind of thing that could be subject to bias or prejudice.

In this way, aesthetic judgement can be motivated by something which is subjective but not relative. This is a starting point, but not yet quite enough. Judgement of taste varies, from my judgement that Poussin is a finer painter of human emotions than his contemporary Le Brun, to my preference for vanilla ice cream over strawberry ice cream. Although both fall under a broadly construed rubric of judgements of taste, they are two different kinds of judgement. This is evident in the fact that I would try to convince others of my judgement in the first case, and I might even consider someone who persisted in the contrary view as perverse or lacking in aesthetic sensibility, whereas I have no view on what kind of ice cream others prefer. In the first type of case, we typically seek agreement with our assessment, in the second we don't. Kant put it in these terms:

> Since it is not grounded in any inclination of the subject (nor in any other underlying interest), but rather the person making the judgement feels himself completely free with regard to the satisfaction that he devotes to the object, he cannot discover as grounds of the satisfaction any private conditions, pertaining to his subject alone, and must therefore regard it as grounded in those that he can also presuppose in everyone else; consequently he must believe himself to have grounds for expecting a similar pleasure of everyone. Hence he will speak of the beautiful as if beauty were a property of the object and the judgement logical…, although it is only aesthetic.

The difference between aesthetic judgement and mere preference, Kant argues, lies in a difference between those pleasures that involve a 'perceptual representation' of the object of pleasure, and those that do not. The latter are cases of sensuous gratification, and these remain subjective and relative. But in the case of taking pleasure in beauty, there is something which the experience is 'about'. That is to say, there is something in the experience different from the experience itself, namely the content of the experience (what philosophers call its intentional content). This is absent in the former case. What marks out the kinds of judgements of taste to which questions of objectivity apply is the fact that they have intentional content.

This does not mean that cases of sensuous gratification are all merely relative. There are people with experienced and nuanced views on food and drink, whose judgements can be trusted: one routinely assumes this in consulting a recipe book, for example. But (allowing for grey areas), if someone does not agree with such views, the best one can say is that there is no accounting for taste, not that there is an error of judgement on the part of someone who disagrees. With judgements of taste involving intentional content, the question of error of judgement is appropriately raised, however, no matter how difficult it might be to resolve in particular cases. Such judgements of taste have a normative ingredient, and they potentially have a universal validity. I say 'potentially' because such assessment is clearly relative to what one thinks works of art are supposed to do. There are challenging genres of art—those which go beyond good stories, good tunes, or naturalistic representations, for example—that will always be ruled out by some as failing to satisfy their own ideas of what art should be doing. Others will dismiss this as a parochial, simple-minded view of art as merely a form of entertainment.

Such disputes about the nature of art presuppose the appropriateness of considerations of objectivity. In particular, we should not assume that there is a correlation between degree of agreement and degree of objectivity, extending from science (high level of agreement), to ethics (middle level of agreement), to aesthetics (significant level of disagreement). Level of agreement has nothing to do with it, and in any case, studies in the history of science have drawn attention to the significant levels of intractable disagreement at various periods in the development of science.

In sum, what are the features that aesthetic objectivity has? Two can be singled out. First, to say that our judgements of taste are objective—or can be assessed against objective standards—is to claim that we think our judgements better than their opposites. As we have seen, this marks out two classes of judgement of taste, for we do not think this of all such judgements, only a special sub-class, characterized by the fact that they have intentional content. Second, my thinking something beautiful doesn't make it beautiful: by contrast with sensual gratification of appetite, for example, when thinking something delicious and its being delicious are just the same thing. Something beautiful (in the sense in which we are talking of beauty here, not in the sense in which we say that a particular person is beautiful) is beautiful in its own right, whether or not our sensibility is sufficiently refined or educated to appreciate this.

Conclusion

As a general characterization of objectivity, I began by describing it as something that requires us to stand back from our perceptions, our beliefs and opinions, to reflect on them, and subject them to a particular kind of scrutiny and judgement: above all, something that requires a degree of indifference in judging that may conflict with our needs and desires. But as we have seen, once we move to specific areas, this needs refinement. In science, for example, what is often at issue is not merely a commitment to comparing one's theories with the evidence, but a sensitivity to questions of what counts as evidence, and an ability to identify arbitrary factors. In daily life, by contrast, removing bias and prejudice from our judgements seems to be paramount, as it does in ethical and aesthetic judgements.

What I hope has come to the fore is that our understanding of objectivity must go beyond definitional questions. There is no simple route to understanding what objectivity is or what it requires of us. One way to approach it in particular cases is to ask: how would I secure objectivity here, or how would I increase the level of objectivity of my judgements? This is not just a practical question, however, and at a theoretical level it might tell us more than simply asking what objectivity is. In many cases, it bears directly on what we want out of objectivity in particular cases, and in that way, it can go to the heart of what we understand by objectivity. In the case of science, for example, the shift from science teaching exclusively in the form of lectures to its teaching through practical laboratory work, whereby one picks up the necessary skills and techniques through a combination of trial and error and professional guidance, is instructive about just what objectivity amounts to in science. Similarly, objectivity in pictorial representations of plants, human anatomy, or particle interactions depends crucially on what one wants these representations for, what one seeks to learn from them. There is some overlap with more everyday decisions here, especially when one is working within a context of risk or uncertainty, but the key aim here is more a question of overcoming prejudice or bias.

There is also a historical dimension to the question, and, if we ignore this, we will fail to grasp the role that objectivity plays in our culture. Many philosophical discussions of objectivity, for example, treat it as a universal and timeless value. But in fact the values of objectivity have come to the centre of everyday life only in the modern era, and these values are to a large extent the result of modern universal educational systems. If we ask how we can make people exercise more objective judgements in regard to political, social, economic, and religious matters, for example, it is to the educational system that one generally has recourse. Objectivity is not merely an intellectual virtue. Rather, it is something that we learn how to achieve, and because it is context-dependent, we learn how to achieve it in context-dependent ways. It is not a one-size-fits-all notion. There is nothing more mistaken than to assume that we can identify an area – science – that manifests objectivity in an archetypal and timeless way, and extrapolate from this to everyday life, lamenting the increasing lack of objectivity as we move further away from the centre.

References

Chapter 1: Introduction

F. de Waal, *Chimpanzee Politics*, revised edn. (Baltimore: The Johns Hopkins University Press, 1998).

S. Gaukroger, *The Emergence of a Scientific Culture* (Oxford: Oxford University Press, 2005), ch. 1.

K. R. Popper, *The Open Society and Its Enemies* (London: Routledge, 1945).

Chapter 2: Is objectivity a form of honesty?

On Wikipedia, see: http://www.slate.com/blogs/blogs/thewrongstuff/archive/2010/07/26/

Hooke's preface to Robert Knox, *An Historical Relation of the Island of Ceylon* (London, 1681), xlvii.

M. de Montaigne, *Complete Works*, ed. D. Frame (Stanford: Stanford University Press, 1980), 151–2.

K. R. Popper, *The Logic of Scientific Discovery*, revised edn. (London: Routledge 1968).

P. Duhem, *To Save the Phenomena: An Essay on the Idea of Physical Theory from Plato to Galileo* (Chicago: University of Chicago Press, 1985).

Galileo, *Dialogue Concerning the Two Chief World Systems – Ptolemaic and Copernican* (Berkeley: University of California Press, 1953), 138–45.

I. Hacking, 'Pull the Other One', *London Review of Books*, 17(2), 26 January 1995; 'Pull the Other One', letter from Richard Pearson, *London Review of Books*, 17(4), 23 February 1995.

Chapter 3: Doesn't science show there is no objectivity?

One of the best general accounts of relativity theory and quantum mechanics is L. Sklar, *Philosophy of Physics* (Oxford: Oxford University Press, 1992).

A. Petersen, *Quantum Physics and the Philosophical Tradition* (Cambridge, Mass.: MIT Press, 1968).

J. Franklin, *Jean Bodin and the Sixteenth Century Revolution in the Methodology of Law and History* (New York: Columbia University Press, 1963).

Chapter 4: Isn't all perception and understanding relative?

J. Annas and J. Barnes, *The Modes of Scepticism: Ancient Texts and Modern Interpretations* (Cambridge: Cambridge University Press, 1985).

T. Nagel, *The View from Nowhere* (Oxford: Oxford University Press, 1986).

Chapter 5: What about our conceptual structuring of the world?

I. Kant, *Critique of Pure Reason* (Cambridge: Cambridge University Press, 1998).

F. Boas, *Anthropology and Modern Life* (New York: Dover, 1988).

E. Sapir, *Language: An Introduction to the Study of Speech* (New York: Harcourt, Brace & Co, 1921).

E. Sapir, 'The Status of Linguistics as a Science', *Language*, 5 (1929).

B. L. Whorf, *Language, Thought, and Reality: Selected Writings of Benjamin Lee Whorf* (Cambridge, Mass.: MIT Press, 1956).

P. Glennie and N. Thrift, *Shaping the Day* (Oxford: Oxford University Press, 2009).

On modularization as an evolutionary response, see D. Fox, 'The Limits of Intelligence', *Scientific American* (July 2011): 20–7.

R. Kurzban, *Why Everyone (Else) is a Hypocrite: Evolution and the Modular Mind* (Princeton: Princeton University Press, 2011).

T. Kuhn, *The Structure of Scientific Revolutions*, 2nd edn. (Chicago: University of Chicago Press, 1962).

I. Lakatos, 'Falsification and the Methodology of Scientific Research Programmes', in I. Lakatos and A. Musgrave (eds.), *Criticism and the Growth of Knowledge* (Cambridge: Cambridge University Press, 1970).

K. R. Popper, *The Logic of Scientific Discovery*, revised edn. (London: Routledge, 1968).

Chapter 6: Is it possible to represent things objectively?

L. Daston, 'Baconian Facts, Academic Civility, and the Prehistory of Objectivity', in A. Megill (ed.), *Rethinking Objectivity* (Durham, NC: Duke University Press, 1994).

H. Putnam, *Reason, Truth and History* (Cambridge: Cambridge University Press, 1981).

S. Gaukroger, 'Justification, Truth, and the Development of Science', *Studies in History and Philosophy of Science*, 29 (1998): 97–112.

L. Daston and P. Galison, *Objectivity* (New York: Zone Books, 2007).

Chapter 7: Objectivity in numbers?

T. M. Porter, *Trust in Numbers: The Pursuit of Objectivity in Science and Public Life* (Princeton: Princeton University Press, 1995).

S. Jenkins, *Thatcher and Sons: A Revolution in Three Acts* (London: Allen Lane, 2006).

Chapter 8: Can the study of human behaviour be objective?

N. Cartwright, *How the Laws of Physics Lie* (Oxford: Oxford University Press, 1983).

P. Harrison, *'Religion' and Religions in the English Enlightenment* (Cambridge: Cambridge University Press, 1990).

T. Masuzawa, *The Invention of World Religions* (Chicago: Chicago University Press, 2005).

S. Prothero, *God Is Not One* (New York: HarperCollins, 2010).

G. Vico, *New Science*, tr. D. Marsh (London: Penguin, 2000).

W. Dilthey, *Selected Writings*, ed. and tr. H. P. Rickman (Cambridge: Cambridge University Press, 1976).

B. H. Smith, *Natural Reflections: Human Cognition at the Nexus of Science and Religion* (New Haven: Yale University Press, 2010).

P. Boyer, *Religion Explained: The Evolutionary Origins of Religious Thought* (New York: Basic Books, 2001).

S. Atran, *In Gods We Trust: The Evolutionary Landscape of Religion* (Oxford: Oxford University Press, 2002).

Chapter 9: Can there be objectivity in ethics?

A. C. Kors, *Atheism in France, 1650–1729* (Princeton: Princeton University Press, 1990).

P. Bayle, *Lettre à M.L.A.D.C. Docteur de Sorbonne, où il est prouvé que les comètes ne sont point le présage d'aucun malheur* (Rotterdam, 1682).

J. Locke, *Essay Concerning Human Understanding*, I.iii.9.

J. Rawls, *A Theory of Justice* (Cambridge, Mass.: Harvard University Press, 1971).

Chapter 10: Can there be objectivity in taste?

D. Hume, 'Of the Standard of Taste', in E. Miller (ed.), *Essays: Moral, Political and Literary* (Indianapolis: Liberty Press, 1985).

I. Kant, *Critique of the Power of Judgment*, ed. P. Guyer (Cambridge: Cambridge University Press, 2000), Part I.

N. Zangwill, *The Metaphysics of Beauty* (Ithaca: Cornell University Press, 2001).

N. Zangwill, 'Aesthetic Judgement', in the online Standard Encyclopedia: http://plato.stanford.edu/entries/aesthetic-judgment/.

Further reading

T. Burge, *Origins of Objectivity* (Oxford: Oxford University Press, 2010).

L. Daston and P. Galison, *Objectivity* (New York: Zone Books, 2007).

D. Dutton, *The Art Instinct* (Oxford: Oxford University Press, 2009).

R. Joyce, *The Myth of Morality* (Cambridge: Cambridge University Press, 2001).

T. Kuhn, *The Structure of Scientific Revolutions* (Chicago: University of Chicago Press, 1962).

I. Lakatos, 'Falsification and the Methodology of Scientific Research Programmes', in I. Lakatos and A. Musgrave (eds.), *Criticism and the Growth of Knowledge* (Cambridge: Cambridge University Press, 1970).

A. Megill (ed.), *Rethinking Objectivity* (Durham, NC: Duke University Press, 1994).

A. W. Moore, *Points of View* (Oxford: Oxford University Press, 1997).

T. Nagel, *The View from Nowhere* (Oxford: Oxford University Press, 1986).

T. M. Porter, *Trust in Numbers: The Pursuit of Objectivity in Science and Public Life* (Princeton: Princeton University Press, 1995).

B. L. Whorf, *Language, Thought, and Reality: Selected Writings of Benjamin Lee Whorf* (Cambridge, Mass.: MIT Press, 1956).

N. Zangwill, *The Metaphysics of Beauty* (Ithaca: Cornell University Press, 2001).

Index

Expand your collection of
VERY SHORT INTRODUCTIONS